C000227228

CHATI
BUILT WARSHIPS SINCE 1860

By Philip MacDougall

Author's Notes

Chatham dockyard is to close in 1984. This was the sad news that greeted the Medway Towns during the Summer of 1981. Not even the more recent Falkland's Crisis has managed to save the yard. So, in 1984, an era will have ended. No more will Royal Navy warships be a regular feature of the Medway's river traffic, whilst the Towns, themselves, will have to confront the spectre of rising unemployment.

First established in the sixteenth century, Chatham is one of the oldest dockyards in the country. Over the years a fine record of building and repairing naval ships has seen the yard go from strength to strength. Now, however, all this is to end. But those who live in the Medway Towns should still be proud of their dockyard. It was from this yard that Nelson's *Victory* was originally launched, whilst iron ship building was furthered by the launch of the *Achilles*.

This particular book deals with the post-1860 period. A period, of course, of rapid change. The earliest vessels mentioned relied upon both steam and sail power, with the *Mersey* (1885) being the first Chatham built warship to abandon a sailing rig. As for the late nineteenth century, this was a time when Chatham was building some of the most powerful ships in the world. Having been completely modernised, Chatham yard was the most advanced of all the dockyards, able to handle all imaginable naval requirements.

The twentieth century witnessed a further change in fortunes. The dockyard, proving itself unable to handle the new Dreadnought class of battleships, went on to specialise in submarine construction work. Over the years, therefore, Chatham went on to build a total of fifty-eight submarines with the last being launched in 1966. At that point the dockyard appeared to be under threat of closure, but was saved by the submarine refit centre that has since allowed Chatham to specialise in refitting the nuclear 'Fleet' class submarines. Additionally, Chatham has undertaken a many frigate refits, whilst the dockyard is also home to the ships of the Standby Squadron.

PHILIP MACDOUGALL
October 1982

INTRODUCTION

By
Rear-Admiral G M K Brewer CB
Flag Officer Medway and
Port Admiral Chatham 1980-1982

As a recent Flag Officer Medway and Port Admiral, Chatham, as well as a Man of Kent, I am very pleased to have the opportunity of writing a short introduction to Philip MacDougall's book.

HM Naval Base Chatham has a long and very distinguished record in the construction of ships, submarines and craft, as well as their refitting and repair, and the readers will find many famous names within these covers. Several have brought back happy memories of my own service in the Royal Navy including HMS HERO of 1858, for I command the Chatham based frigate HMS JUNO which starred in the BBC 'WARSHIP' series as a more modern 'HERO', I have also command the frigate HMS GRENVILLE which, although not built here, was given a major conversion to her new anti-submarine role at Chatham..

The variety of talent and skill displayed by the generations of local people, and some from further afield, who have worked in the Chatham Naval Base over the centuries is unique and their loyalty to the Nation and the Royal Navy is unsurpassed. While I am, of course, sad to see the Base close, as a Naval Officer I am glad to know that much of this expertise will be transferred to HM Naval Bases Devonport and Rosyth, as part of their build up in readiness to take over tasks previously carried out at Chatham.

This book will serve as a timely reminder of the debt owed to Chatham and with whom I am proud to have been associated.

George mac Brewer

ORPHEUS   'Jason' class wooden screw corvette

2,365 tons; 225' x 40' 8" x 19'; 11 knots; complement 240;
Armament 16 x 8" ML SB, 1 x 7" ML SB, 4 x 40 pdr BL.

Laid down May 1858; launched 23 June 1860.

A composite vessel, fitted with a telescopic funnel and hoisting screws, *Orpheus* was commissioned in 1861 for the Australian station. Leaving Spithead on December 5, 1862, she was never to reach her destination. Striking the Manukau Bar, off New Zealand (February 2, 1863) the vessel was completely wrecked, with the loss of 22 officers and 157 men.

ATLAS   91-gun wooden screw second rate battleship

5260 tons; 245' x 55 6";
Armament 34 x 8" ML SB, 1 x 68 pdr BL, 56 x 32 pdr BL.

Laid down June 1858; launched 21 July, 1860.
Although launched in July 1860, the *Atlas,* a traditional timber built man-of-war, was never completed. Developments in naval warfare, and the emergence of the iron clad had made her obsolete.
1863   Laid-up, Sheerness.
1884   November, lent Metropolitan Asylum Board.
1904   Broken-up.

UNDAUNTED   'Immortalite' class wooden screw frigate

4094 tons; 250' x 52' x 22¾'; 13 knots; complement 550.
Armament 30 x 8" ML SB, 20 x 32 pdrs ML SB, 1 x 68 pdr ML SB.

Laid down May 1859; launched January 1, 1861.
A composite vessel, fitted with a telescopic funnel and hoisting screws, the *Undaunted* was ship rigged throughout. Once described as the finest example of a wooden hulled screw frigate.
1861   January. Not immediately completed. She was, instead, laid up at Sheerness. Remained there until 1875.
1875   March 2. Commissioned for East Indies. Serving as flagship, she was the last wooden vessel to carry an admiral's flag.
1879   Returned to Chatham and paid off.
1882   Sold.

RATTLESNAKE   **'Jason' class wooden screw corvette.**

2,431 tons; 225' x 40½' x 19'; 11½ knots; complement 240.
Armament 20 x 8" ML SB, 1 x 110 pdr.

Laid down March, 1859; launched 9 July, 1861.
A composite vessel, ship rigged. The 110-pdr Armstrong breech loader was
removed in 1864 following a series of firing accidents.

1862	16 August. Commissioned for West coast of Africa.
1866	Refitting at Devonport.
1867	8 September. Commissioned for second tour of duty off the West coast of Africa.
1873	13 August. Bombarded the Ashante town of Chamah as retribution for an attack upon a British policing force.
1874	Arrived back at Devonport and paid off.
1880	August. Placed on sale list.

ROYAL OAK   **Wooden Broadside Ironclad**

6,366 tons; 273' x 58' x 24'; 12½ knots; complement 585.
Armament (1863) 11 x 7" BL, 24 x 68 pdrs ML;
              (1867 after re-arming) 4 x 8" ML, 20 x 7" ML.

Laid down 1 May, 1860; launched 10 September 1862.
The navy's first wooden hulled armoured ship, the *Royal Oak* was originally
designed as a 91-gun two decker. Reduced by one deck, lengthened by 21' and
given 4½" armouring she was eventually barque rigged with a 25,000 sq. ft. sail
area. Machinery supplied by Maudslay.

1861	14 May. Decision to convert whilst still on stocks.
1863	Steamed or towed to Devonport.
	Commissioned for the Mediterranean.
1867	Paid-off for rearming. Returned to Channel service, but in collision with *Warrior*. Devonport for essential hull repairs.
1869	April. Commissioned for Mediterranean.
	November. Grounded outside Port Said during opening of Suez Canal. Towed off by *Lord Warden*.
1871	December. Paid-off at Portsmouth. Planned refit eventually cancelled. Placed in fourth-class reserve.
1885	30 September. Sold to Castle for breaking up.

SALAMIS   Paddle despatch vessel.

929 tons; 220' x 28' x 11'; 14 knots; complement 68.
Armament 2 x 9 pdr.

Laid down 9 September, 1861; launched 19 May, 1863.

1865	May. Commissioned for 'Particular Service'. Operating against Chinese pirates, destroying eight craft on December 12.
1867	January. Commissioned for China.
1874	Paid off at Devonport.
1876	29 August. Commissioned for Mediterranean.
1879	October. Joined Channel Squadron.
1883	Paid off at Sheerness. Remained for breaking up.

ACHILLES   Broadside Ironclad

9,820 tons; 380' x 58' 3" x 27' 3"; 14 knots; complement 709.
Armament (1864) 20 x 100 pdrs ML (6 x 68 pdr ML added in 1865)
          (1868) 22 x 7" ML, 4 x 8" ML
          (1874) 14 x 9" ML, 2 x 7" ML.

Laid down 1 August 1861; undocked 23 December 1863.
First iron built warship to be constructed in a royal dockyard. Stepping four masts, only British warship ever to do so, she carried a total sail area of 44,000 sq. ft. Reduced to three masts in 1865.

1864	September. Commissioned for Channel Squadron.
1868	Paid off and rearmed.
1869	July. Commissioned at Chatham as guardship of the First Reserve in the Portland district.
1874	Paid off and rearmed.
1875	December. Commissioned as First Reserve guardship of the Liverpool district.
1877	17 May. Commissioned for Channel Squadron.
1878	Despatched to Mediterranean. In that year she passed through the Dardanelles with Admiral Hornby.
1879	October. Collided with *Alexandria* and sustained an underwater leak.
1880	Returned to Channel Squadron.
1885	Paid off at Devonport.
1898	Held at Portsmouth but inactive.
1901	August. Arrived Malta. Harbour duty as depot ship.
1902	Re-named *Hibernia*.
1904	March. Re-named *Egmont*.
1918	June. Re-named *Pembroke*.
1923	26 January. Sold to Granton Shipbreaking Company.

HMS ACHILLES (1863)

BELLEROPHON   Central battery ironclad.

7,551 tons; 300' x 56' x 24' x 8"; 14 knots; complement 650.
Armament (1866) 10 x 9" ML, 5 x 7" ML
          (1885) 10 x 8" BL, 4 x 6" BL, 6 x 4" BL, 2 x TC (16" Whiteheads).
A prototype central battery ship, the *Bellerophon* was only the second iron
hulled warship to be built in a royal dockyard. Constructed in No. 2 dock, she
was laid down as soon as the *Achilles* was floated out.

Laid down 23 December, 1863, launched 26 April, 1865.

1866	March. Commissioned for Channel Squadron.
1868	Collided with *Minotaur* whilst manoeuvring in Belfast Lough. Armour frames driven in, but leaking confined.
1871	Transferred to Mediterranean.
1872	Received a major refit at Chatham.
1873	October. Commissioned as flagship to the North American and West Indies station. Whilst proceeding to her new command, she was accidentally rammed by the steamer *Flamsteed*. At the time, the two vessels had been involved in passing mail. The *Flamsteed* stove in her own bows and subsequently sunk.
1880	Paid-off and refitted at Devonport.
1885	15 December. Commissioned for the North American and West Indies station flying, in succession, the flags of Admirals the Earl of Clanwilliam, Lyons and Watson.
1891	Paid off.
1892	30 April. Commissioned as Port Guardship, Pembroke Dock.
1895-1903	Devonport Reserve.
1904	Relegated to harbour service. Stokers' training ship *Indus III*. Conversion work carried out by Palmers.
1922	12 December. Sold to P. and W. McClellan. Broken up during 1923.

LORD WARDEN   'Lord Clyde' class ironclad.

7,842 tons; 280' x 59' x 27'; 13½ knots; complement 605.
Armament 2 x 9" ML; 14 x 8" ML, 2 x 7" ML, 2 x 20 pdrs BL.

Laid down 24 December 1963; launched 27 May, 1865.
Timber hulled, with additional 4½" armouring, the *Lord Warden* was constructed as a means of using up dockyard timber that had been accumulated
over the past twenty years. The largest wooden ship built for the Royal Navy,
and the last true broadside.

1867	July. Commissioned at Chatham for Channel service.
1868-75	Mediterranean. Flagship from March 1869.
1875-76	Portsmouth for refit.
1876	12 December. Commissioned as guardship of the First Reserve in the Forth.
1878	Joined 'Particular Service Squadron' during Russian war scare, and then returned to former duties off Queensferry.
1884	Fitted with Whitehead torpedo carriages and given net defences.
1886	December. Paid off.
1889	Broken up. Her timbers were found to be in a first class condition.

HMS LORD WARDEN (1865)

REINDEER   'Cameleon' class wooden screw sloop.

1,365 tons 185' x 33' x 14' 8"; 9 knots; complement 180;
Armament 5 x 40 pdr ML SB, 12 x 32 pdr ML SB.

Laid down May 1860; launched 29 March 1866.
Built for cruising in open water rather than coastal work, all 'Cameleon' class
sloops were fitted with telescopic funnels and hoisting screws. The *Reindeer*
was originally cancelled in May 1865, but construction work was resumed prior
to the vessel being removed from stocks.

1866	October. Commissioned for the Pacific.
1871	Refit at Portsmouth.
1871-74	Pacific duties resumed.
1875	Paid off at Sheerness.
1876	December. Broken up at Chatham.

MYRMIDON   'Cormorant' class wooden screw gunvessel.

877 tons; 185' x 28½' x 11'; 10 knots; complement 90;
Armament 1 x 110 BL, 1 x 68 pdr SB, 2 x 20 pdr.

Launched 5 June, 1867; completed October, 1867 (as survey vessel).

1867	29 October. Commissioned at Chatham for Cape and West Coast.
1870-72	North American and West Indies station.
1872-77	Pacific.
1878	January. Paid off at Chatham.
1884	10 January. Commissioned at Sheerness for survey duties.
1888-89	Continuing survey work off China.
1889	Sold at Hong Kong.

BLANCHE   'Eclipse' class wooden screw corvette.

1,682 tons; 212' x 36' x 16½'; 13½ knots; complement 180;
Armament 2 x 7" ML, 4 x 64 pdr ML

Launched 17 August, 1867; completed January 1868.
Originally laid down as a sloop, but later re-designated a corvette.

1868	15 January. Commissioned for Australia.
	September. Shelled villages on Solomon Islands as a punitive measure.
1875	Paid off at Sheerness.
1877	4 September. Commissioned for North America and West Indies.
1885	Paid off at Chatham.
1886	March. Placed on sales list and subsequently sold.

HMS HERCULES (1868)

HERCULES   Central battery ironclad.

8,677 tons; 325′ x 59′ x 24′; 14½ knots; complement 638;
Armament 8 x 10″ ML, 2 x 9″ ML, 4 x 7″ ML.

Laid down 1 February, 1866; launched 10 February 1868.
An enlarged *Bellerophon.* Included more powerful engines and heavier guns.

1868	Commissioned for Channel service.
1871	Successfully towed the *Agincourt* off Pearl Rock, Gibraltar.
1872	Collided with and badly damaged *Northumberland* at Funchal.
1874	Paid off at Portsmouth and refitted prior to relieving the *Lord Warden* as flag ship in the Mediterranean.
1875-77	Admiral Drummond's flag ship in the Mediterranean. Paid off at Portsmouth.
1878	Flagship of Admiral Cooper Key's 'Particular Service Squadron' then being assembled at Portland. Torpedo carriages added.
1879-81	Guardship in Clyde.
1881-90	Flagship of Reserve Fleet. During this period a Baltic cruise was undertaken, whilst net defences were added in 1886.
1892-93	Ineffectual modernisation programme undertaken. During this period she was re-engined, re-boilered and two 6″ QFs replaced her forward pair of 7″ MLs. Additionally, six 4.7″ QFs were placed on her upper decks and a range of smaller guns scattered on her top sides. All sails were removed at this time. Basically, though, the vessel was obsolete, and no amount of modernisation could overcome this simple problem.
1893-94	Held in Reserve at Portsmouth.
1904	Temporary harbour flagship of Portsmouth C-in-C.
1905-15	Depot ship at Gibraltar and re-named *Calcutta* in 1909.
1915	Re-named *Fisguard II* and became artificer training ship at Portsmouth. By now a totally unrecognisable roofed-in hulk.
1932	July. Sold Messrs Ward and stripped at Morecambe. 1 December. Arrived Preston for breaking up.

11

BEACON   Name ship of class of composite twin screw gun vessels.

603 tons; 155′ x 25′ x 9′; 9½ knots; complement 80;
Armament 1 x 7″ ML, 1 x 64 pdr ML, 2 x 20 pdr BL.

Laid down 31 January, 1867; launched 17 August, 1867.
Early example of a composite structure. Designed with a shallow draught and heavy armament.

1868	15 January. Commissioned at Sheerness for South America.
1875	December. Ordered to Brazil.
1878	January. To Devonport for refit.
1879	23 January. Commissioned at Chatham for East Indies.
1882	13 July. Following bombardment of Alexandria, she steamed into the harbour and landed a number of marines to keep order ashore. August. Assisted in patrolling Suez Canal following its return to British hands.
1883	21 September. Helped in blockading the Nile during the Arab rebellion.
1885	Paid off at Chatham.
1888	December. Sold for breaking up.

MONARCH   Ironclad Battleship.

8,320 tons; 330′ x 57½′ x 24¼′; 15 knots; complement 575;
Armament (1869) 4 x 12″ ML, 3 x 7″ ML
(1871) 4 x 12″ ML, 2 x 9″ ML, 1 x 7″ ML.

Laid down 1 June, 1866; launched 25 May, 1868.
The first sea going capital ship to be armed on the centre line principal.

1869	May. Commissioned at Chatham for Channel Squadron. Re-armed at end of commission.
1874	June. Re-commissioned for Channel Squadron.
1878	16 April. Commissioned at Chatham for Mediterranean. Torpedo launchers added earlier in year.
1882	11 July. Commenced bombardment action against the water front batteries of Alexandria. Expended 300 shells. This was the high point in her Mediterranean years, as she spent most of her time in harbour owing to fuel restrictions.
1885	March. Broke down whilst at sea. Paid off and re-fitted at Malta. Returned to Portsmouth. 15 September. Commissioned for Channel Squadron.
1887	Attended Spithead review.
1890	Paid off for long refit. Re-engined, given lower masts and new bridge. 4 x 12 pdr QFs and 10 x 3 pdr QFs added to existing armament.
1892-96	Chatham Reserve.
1897	26 January. Commissioned at Chatham as Guardship for Cape Town.
1904	March. Re-named *Simoon* and became a depot ship at Simonstown.
1905	Brought home and sold to the Garnham shipbreaking company on April 4.

SULTAN   Ironclad Battleship.

9,290 tons; 325′ x 59′ x 26′ 5″; 14 knots; complement 633;
Armament 8 x 10″ ML, 4 x 9″ ML, 7 x 20 pdrs BL.

Laid down 29 February, 1868; undocked 31 May, 1870.

1871	Commissioned at Chatham for Channel Squadron.
1876	Refit, followed by her commissioning for the Mediterranean.
1879	Refitted, with 7 x 4″ BLs, 4 x 6 pdr QFs and 4 x 14″ TCs added. Also re-boilered. Reduced to Reserve at Portsmouth.
1882	20 April. Commissioned at Portsmouth for Channel Squadron. Detached to re-inforce Mediterranean. Present at bombardment of Alexandria. Sustained hit in forecastle battery.
1889	6 March. Grounded and later sank on an unchartered rock in South Comino Channel, Malta. Salvaged. Returned to Portsmouth and placed in reserve.
1893	Re-constructed. Re-boilered and 4″ guns replaced by 4.7″ QFs. Returned to Reserve.
1906	Reduced to artificers training ship and given name *Fisguard IV*.
1932	Reverted to original name, having become a mechanical repair ship.
1940	Depot ship for Portsmouth minesweepers.
1946	October. Broken up at Dalmuir.

GLATTON   Coast Defence Ship.

4,910 tons; 245′ x 54′ x 19′; 12 knots; complement 185;
Armament 2 x 12″ ML, 3 x 6 pdr.

Laid down 10 August, 1868; launched 8 March, 1871.
The first British single turret ship, *Glatton* was intended for both coast defence and attacking enemy coastal defences. As is so often the case, she was a poor compromise. Having a deep draught and low free board, she was not really suited for either of these duties.

1872	May. Commissioned into Dockyard Reserve at Portsmouth.
1878	Joined the 'Particular Service Squadron' at Portland. Returned to Portsmouth Reserve in August.
1881	Fitted with 14″ torpedo carriages.
1887	During manouvres of that year she was involved for defending the Thames estuary. Only recorded time at sea.
1889	Reduced to Second Class Reserve.
1903	July. Sold.

WOODLARK   'Plover' class twin screw gun vessel.

755 tons; 170' x 29' x 10'; 10 knots; complement 90;
Armament 1 x 7 ML, 2 x 40 pdr BL.

Laid down May, 1870; launched 9 March, 1871.
The 'Plover' class were the last wooden gun vessels built for the Royal Navy.
Also the smallest vessels built with telescopic funnels.

1872	Commissioned for North America and West Indies station.
1877	Held at Devonport.
1880	16 March. Commissioned for East Indies.
1887	9 March. Sold at Bombay.

SCOURGE   'Ant' class Iron screw gun boat.

254 tons; 85' x 26' x 6'; 8½ knots; complement 30;
Armament 1 x 10" ML.

Laid down 25 August, 1870; launched 25 March, 1871.

1873-84	At Portsmouth but not in commission.
1884-1903	At Devonport. Tender to *Defiance.*
1904	Service as dockyard tank vessel. Re-named C.79.

SNAKE   'Ant' class Iron screw gun boat.

254 tons; 85' x 26' x 6'; 8½ knots; complement 30;
Armament 1 x 10" ML.

Laid down 25 August, 1870; launched 25 March, 1871.

1873-84	At Portsmouth but not in commission.
1884-1901	Tender to *Excellent.*
1902-07	Laid up. Portsmouth.
1907	23 September. Completed as dockyard cable lighter YC15.

FROLIC   Name ship of class of twin screw gun vessels.

610 tons; 155' x 25' x 7¾'; 10½ knots; complement 80;
Armament 1 x 7" ML, 1 x 64 pdr ML, 2 x 20 pdr BL.

Launched 29 February, 1872.
The 'Frolic' class consisted of just four vessels. All were built at Chatham.

1872	Commissioned for China station.
1880	July. Returned to Chatham and paid off.
1883	26 July. Commissioned at Sheerness for Cape and West Coast.
1885	Transferred to South-East coast of America.
1886	December. To Devonport and paid off.
1888	January. Transferred to Thames as drillship for RNA Volunteers.
1893	January. At Sheerness for conversion to Coast Guard vessel. Re-named WV.30 *Roach River.*
1897	Became WV.41 *Roach River.*
1908	April. Sold.

KESTREL   'Frolic' class twin screw gun vessel.

610 tons; 155' x 25' x 7¾'; 10½ knots; complement 80;
Armament 1 x 7" ML, 1 x 64 pdr ML, 2 x 20 pdr BL.

Launched 29 February, 1872.
1873   8 January. Commissioned for China station.
1885   Returned to Chatham and paid off.
1888   Sold.

RUPERT   Coast Defence Ship.

5,444 tons; 250' x 53' x 22½'; 13½ knots; complement 217;
Armament (1874) 2 x 10" ML, 2 x 64 pdr ML
         (1887) 2 x 6" BL, 2 x 10" ML, 4 x 4 pdr QF, 4 x TT
         (1892) 2 x 9.2" BL, 2 x 6" BL, 4 x 6 pdr QF, 4 x TT.

Laid down 6 June, 1870; floated out 12 March, 1872.
An iron armoured turret ship, fitted with a ram and having greater manoeuver-
ability than the poorly designed *Glatton*.
1874-76   Held at Chatham.
1876   25 May. Commissioned for Mediterranean.
1882   Portsmouth Reserve.
1885   April. Joined 'Particular Service Squadron' being assembled at
          Portland. Returned to Portsmouth in August when she was
          commissioned as port guardship at Hull.
1887   Rearmed.
1890   March. Reserve at Portsmouth.
1891-93   Rearmed and given new machinery.
1893   5 July. Commissioned at Devonport as guardship at Pembroke
          dockyard.
1895   12 December. Commissioned at Devonport for Mediterranean.
1902   Devonport Reserve.
1904   Portguard ship, Bermuda.
1907   7 October. Sold in Bermuda.

FIDGET   'Ant' class iron screw gunboat.

254 tons; 85' x 26' x 6'; 8½ knots; complement 30;
Armament 1 x 10" ML.

Laid down September, 1871; floated out 12 March, 1872.
Never placed in commission. Held at Portsmouth until 1905 when she was
hulked. Built in No. 2 dock at the same time as *Rupert*.

BADGER   'Ant' class iron screw gunboat.

254 tons; 85′ x 26′ x 6′; 8½ knots; complement 30;
Armament 1 x 10″ ML.

Launched 13 March, 1872.

1872-95	Held at Portsmouth. Not in commission.
1899	Tender to *Cambridge*, the Devonport Gunnery School.
1905	Devonport. Paid off.
1908	October. Sold to Loveridge and Co. of Hartlepool.

READY   'Frolic' class twin screw gun vessel.

610 tons; 155′ x 25′ x 7¾′; 10½ knots; complement 80;
Armament 1 x 7″ ML, 1 x 64 pdr ML, 2 x 20 pdr BL.

Laid down February, 1872; launched 24 September, 1872.

1873	Commissioned for South-East coast of America.
1878	Commissioned at Sheerness for East Indies.
1884	January. Commissioned at Bermuda for North American and West Indies station.
1888	January. Commissioned at Bermuda for North American and West Indies station.
1892	At Bermuda for conversion to dockyard tank vessel.
1894	Jamaica dockyard. Re-named *Drudge* in 1916.
1920	February. Sold at Bermuda.

RIFLEMAN   'Frolic' class twin screw gun vessel.

610 tons; 155′ x 25′ x 7¾′; 10½ knots; complement 80;
Armament 1 x 7″ ML, 1 x 64 pdr ML, 2 x 20 pdr BL.

Laid down February, 1872; launched 20 November, 1872.

1873	Commissioned for East Indies, being involved in the landing of a small party on the coast of Baluchistan for purposes of protecting an Indo-European company telegraph station.
1874	December. Involved in the suppression of a native rebellion that broke out in Mombasa.
1876	April. Ordered home.
1885	Commissioned at Sheerness for Cape and West Coast.
1889	Returned to Sheerness and laid up.
1890	April. Sold for breaking up.

ARIEL   Name ship of class of single screw gunboats.

438 tons; 125' x 23' x 8½'; 10 knots; complement 60;
Armament 2 x 64 pdr ML, 2 x 20 pdr BL.

Laid down February, 1872; launched 11 February, 1873.

1873   July. Shortly after completion she collided with timber in the River Medway and had to return to Chatham for repairs to her screw. Later in the year she was dispatched to the Cape and West Coast station.

1876   1 July. Participated in blockade of Dahomey following attacks on British subjects at Whydah.

1877   26 November. Returned to UK, subsequently re-commissioned for Coastguard duties.

1889   August. Sold for breaking up.

ZEPHYR   'Ariel' class single screw gunboat.

438 tons; 125' x 23' x 8½'; 10 knots; complement 60;
Armament 2 x 64 pdr ML, 2 x 20 pdr BL.

Laid down March, 1872; launched 11 February, 1873.

1873-80   North American and West Indies station.

1880   At Chatham for paying off.
       6 October. Commissioned at Sheerness for China station.

1889   August. Sold.

ALBATROSS   'Fantome' class single screw sloop.

950 tons; 160' x 31' x 12½'; 10½ knots; complement 120;
Armament 2 x 7" ML, 2 x 64 pdr ML.

Laid down May, 1873; launched 24 July, 1873.

1874   14 February. Commissioned at Chatham for Pacific.

1879   23 October. Commissioned at Chatham for China Station.

1886   Paid off at Chatham.

1889   February. Broken up at Chatham.

FLYING FISH   'Fantome' class single screw sloop.

950 tons; 160' x 31' x 12½'; 11½ knots; complement 120;
Armament 2 x 7" ML, 2 x 64 pdr ML.

Launched 27 November, 1873.

1874   18 June. Commissioned at Chatham for East Indies. Engaged in suppression of slave trade.

1878   Converted as survey ship.

1880   After a refit at Sheerness, she was commissioned for survey duties in the Far East.

1886   Ordered home and sold December, 1888.

HMS RALEIGH (1873)

RALEIGH Frigate.

5,200 tons; 298′ x 49′ x 24½′; 15½ knots; complement 530;
Armament (1874) 2 x 9″ ML chasers, 14 x 7″ ML, 6 x 6″ ML
      (1884) 2 x 9″ ML, 7 x 7″ ML, 8 x 6″ BL, 8 x 5″ BL, 2 x 16″ TT.

Laid down 1871; launched 1 March, 1873.
Designed for speed, the *Raleigh* had relatively little armouring and powerful
6,000 h.p. engine. Proved expensive to run, and was frequently used under sail.
As such, she was the Navy's last ship to round the Horn under sail.

1874	13 January. Commissioned for the Flying Squadron, being placed under the command of Captain George Tryon. Cruising off the Cape of Good Hope.
1878	1 January. Recommissioned at Malta.
	July. Participated in occupation of Cyprus.
1879	December. Trooping to Australia under March 1880.
1881	Paid off, Devonport.
1884	Partially rearmed.
1885	Commissioned at Devonport as flagship of Cape and West Coast Squadron.
1895	Returned to Devonport and paid off.
1898	Commissioned for sail training squadron.
1902	Portsmouth to pay off.
1905	July. Sold to Ward's of Morecambe and broken up.

HMS ALEXANDRA (1875)

ALEXANDRA   Central battery ironclad.

9,490 tons; 325' x 64' x 26¼'; 15 knots; complement 674;
Armament (1877) 2 x 11" ML, 10 x 10" ML, 6 x 20 pdr BL
            (1891) 4 x 9.2" BL, 8 x 10" ML, 6 x 4" BL
            (1897) 4 x 9.2" BL, 8 x 10" ML, 6 x 4.7" QF.

Laid down 5 March, 1873; launched 7 April, 1875.
Originally laid down as *Superb,* but her launch by the future Queen Alexandra
prompted a change of name. An improved *Sultan* she was, at the time of her
completion, the fastest battleship afloat. This resulted from her being fitted
with two cylinder Vertical Inverted Compound engines, the first Royal Navy
ship to receive such machinery. *Alexandra* was not only the last British central
battery ship, but was also considered the most successful.

1877	2 January. Commissioned at Chatham as Mediterranean flagship.
1878	As flagship of Vice-Admiral Hornby she was at the head of six ships which cleared for action and proceeded through the Dardanelles to Constantinople to protect British interests during the conflict between Russia and Turkey. Amongst other vessels in this squadron were the Chatham built *Achilles* and *Temeraire.*
1880	Involved in a collision with *Achilles.* Later that year she was paid off at Malta, and then re-commissioned with a new crew.
1882	July. Flying the flag of Admiral Sir Frederick Beauchamp Seymour, she lay off Alexandria leading a fleet of 14 ships.
	11 July. At 7 a.m. she fired the first shot in the bombardment of

19

HMS ALEXANDRA (continued)

Alexandria which was not to cease until 5 p.m. Received 24 hits from shot or shell outside her armour, and was struck, in all, about 60 times.

August. Marines from the *Alexandra* assisted in the seizure and control of the Suez Canal.

September. Contributed men and machine guns to the naval brigade subsequently involved in the attack on Tel-el-Kebir.

1884	Whilst undergoing a short refit at Malta, her 20 pdr guns were removed, and replaced by 4-inch BLs.
1885	Contributed to the naval brigade which took part in the battles of Abu Klea and Metemmeh.
1886	Paid off, but re-commissioned with a new crew. Flagship to the Duke of Edinburgh.
1887-88	Amongst those serving on board the *Alexandra* at this time was H.R.H. Prince George of Wales, the future King George V. His rank was that of lieutenant.
1889-90	Returned to Chatham and subsequently re-constructed, being re-rigged with fighting tops. Also rearmed.
1891	Became flagship to Reserve Fleet at Portland.
1901-04	Chatham Reserve.
1905	Laid up at Kyle-of-Bute.
1908	October. Sold to Garnham for £21,750.

TEMERAIRE   Ironclad with central battery and barbette mounted guns.

8,540 tons; 285′ x 62′ x 27′; 14½ knots; complement 580;
Armament 4 x 11″ ML, 4 x 10″ ML, 4 x 20 pdr BL.

Laid down 18 August, 1873; launched 9 May, 1876.
An experimental design, two of her 11″ guns were mounted in barbettes and upon special disappearing carriages structured on the Moncrieff principle. Other large guns mounted in central battery formation.

1877	1 August. Commissioned at Chatham for Mediterranean.
1878	Passed into Dardanelles with Admiral Hornby's squadron.
1882	Played a leading part at the bombardment of Alexandria when she fired 220 shells and silenced Fort Mex.
1884	Refitted at Malta. Her 20-pdrs replaced by six 4″ BLs, four 6-pdr QFs and ten 3-pdr QFs. Upon recommissioning served, for a short time, as flag ship to the Duke of Edinburgh.
1887	Paid off at Portsmouth and served with Channel squadron during the winter period.
1888	Returned to Mediterranean. Involved in collision with *Orion*.
1891	June. Paid off at Devonport and entered Reserve.
1902	July. Commissioned at Devonport as Depot Ship for Fleet Reserve.
1904	April. Re-named *Indus II*, training ship.
1915	January. Re-named *Akbar*.
1921	May. Sold to Rijsdÿk Ship Breaking Company.

GARNET 'Emerald' class composite single screw corvette.

2,120 tons; 220' x 40' x 18'; 13 knots; complement 230;
Armament 12 x 64 pdr ML (later rearmed with 14 x 5" BL).

Laid down March, 1875; launched 30 June, 1876.

1878	Commissioned at Chatham for South-East coast of America.
1882	Paid off at Sheerness.
	September. Commissioned for South-East coast of America.
1887	Paid off at Sheerness.
	23 August. Commissioned for East Indies.
1890	1 November. Commissioned at Malta for Pacific.
1895	April. Paid off at Chatham and subsequently laid up.
1899	October. At Devonport for conversion to coal hulk.
1904	December. Sold.

EURYALUS 'Bacchante' class single screw frigate.

3,932 tons; 280' x 45½' x 23¼'; 14½ knots; complement 375;
Armament 16 x 7" ML, 2 x 6" ML (two of the 7" MLs later replaced by 6" BLs)

Laid down 1 November, 1873; launched 31 January, 1877.

1878	6 June. Commissioned at Chatham as flagship for East Indies.
1882	August. Disembarked men for securing the, then threatened, Suez Canal.
1885	December. Paid off.
1897	May. Sold to Cohen, Blackwall.

AGAMEMNON Battleship.

8,510 tons; 280' x 66' x 23½'; 13 knots; complement 345;
Armament 4 x 12" ML, 2 x 6" BL, 6 x 6 pdr QF, 2 x TC.

Laid down 9 May, 1876; launched 17 September, 1879.
Designed during a period of extreme naval economies, the *Agamemnon* was a comparatively small vessel and one of the last to be armed with muzzle loading guns. Her shallow draught allowed her to operate more efficiently in the Baltic and Black Sea.

1883	April. Ordered to Devonport as a drill ship.
1884	September. Commissioned for duties in China. While on passage ran aground in Suez Canal.
1886	March. Mediterranean. Stern altered in Malta dockyard in an effort to correct erratic steering.
1888	Blockaded Zanzibar littoral in an effort to suppress slavery.
1889	Feb-Nov. East India station. Part of blockade fleet during anti-slavery operations off Zanzibar.
1889-90	With Mediterranean Fleet.
1892	October. Paid off into Devonport Reserve.
1902	July. Placed on sales list. Sold for scrap in 1903.

HMS CORMORANT (1877)

CORMORANT   **'Osprey' class composite single screw sloop.**

1,130 tons; 170' x 36' x 15¾'; 11½ knots; complement 140;
Armament 2 x 7" ML, 4 x 64 pdr ML.

Laid down August, 1876; launched 12 September, 1877.

1878	Commissioned at Chatham for Australia.
1879	Involved in punitive expedition against natives of New Hebrides.
1883	Paid off at Portsmouth.
1885	Commissioned at Portsmouth for Pacific.
1889	Paid off at Gibraltar.
1891	Tender to base ship, Gibraltar.
1894	Commissioned at Gibraltar as Base Ship.
1946	Re-named *Rooke*.
1949	Broken up at Malaga, Spain.

DOTEREL   Name ship of class of single screw sloops.

1,130 tons; 170' x 36' x 15¾'; 6 knots; complement 140;
Armament 2 x 7" ML, 4 x 64 pdr ML.

Laid down 13 May, 1878; launched 2 March, 1880.

1880	Commissioned at Chatham for South Pacific.
1881	26 April. Blown up by accident off Punta Arenas, Chile.

The *Doterel*, on her way to relieve the *Penguin*, had been carrying out soundings along the Patagonian coast when she suffered an internal explosion which resulted in the loss of 143 lives.

CONSTANCE   'Comus' class single screw steel sloop.

2,380 tons; 225' x 44½' x 19¼'; 13½ knots; complement 265;
Armament 2 x 7" ML, 12 x 64 pdr ML.

Laid down 1878; launched 9 June, 1880.
The 'Comus' class were the first cruisers, of less than 3,000 tons, to be given metal hulls.

1882	3 October. Commissioned at Chatham for China.
1886	17 January. Recommissioned at Hong Kong.
1889	Devonport. Paid off.
1899	15 December. Sold to King (of Garston.)

POLYPHEMUS   Torpedo Ram.

2,640 tons; 240' x 40' x 20½'; 18 knots; complement 146;
Armament 5 x 14" TT, 6 x 1" (later replaced by 2 x 6 pdr)

Laid down 21 September, 1878; launched 15 June, 1881.
Designed for torpedo attack, the *Polyphemus* had an additional spur ram. Heavily armoured with a high turn of speed.

1882	16 February. Due to threatened hostilities in the Mediterranean she was commissioned for a newly assembled Special Service Squadron.
1885	30 June. During annual manoeurvres she was responsible for destruction of Berehaven boom. Her ram remaining undamaged.
1886	Commissioned for Mediterranean. Remained until 1900.
1903	July. Sold.

HMS CONQUEROR (1881)

CONQUEROR   Name ship of class of turret ram battleships.

6,200 tons; 270′ x 58′ x 22′; 14 knots; complement 330;
Armament 2 x 12″ BL, 4 x 6″ BL, 7 x 6 pdr QF.

Laid down 28 April, 1879; undocked 8 September, 1881.
A small, single turret battleship, the *Conqueror* was an improved *Rupert,* with more powerful guns and greater coal endurance. A large underwater ram demonstrates the navy's continued reliance upon this particular weapon. Not considered a successful design, however.

1887	5 July. Commissioned at Chatham for the Jubilee review.
	September. Joined Devonport Reserve.
1889	Became tender to gunnery school *Cambridge.*
1902	Paid off and eventually laid up at Holy Loch.
1907	9 April. Sold to Castle for £16,800.

HMS WARSPITE (1884)

CALYPSO 'Calliope' class steel corvette.

2,770 tons; 235′ x 44½′ x 20′; 14 knots; complement 317;
Armament 4 x 6″ BL, 12 x 5″ BL, 2 x TC.

Laid down 1881; launched 7 June, 1883.
Similar to the 'Comus' class, but with an extended armoured deck. One of the
more successful cruiser designs of this period.

1885	21 September. Commissioned at Chatham. Training squadron until about 1896.
1898-1902	Devonport. Paid off.
1902	Training ship (Newfoundland government until 1922).
1916	15 February. Re-named *Briton*.
1922	7 April. Sold as store hulk.

WARSPITE 'Imperieuse' class armed cruiser.

8,400 tons; 315′ x 62′ x 26¾′; 18 knots; complement 555;
Armament 4 x 9.2″ BL, 10 x 6″ BL, 4 x 6 pdr QF, 6 x 18″ TT.

Laid down 25 October, 1881; launched 29 January, 1884.
Not considered a particularly successful design, being overweight and consequently having a low draught. Guns mounted within individual barbettes.

1888-90	Not completed until June 1888, *Warspite* continued fitting out until 1890.
1890	14 February. Commissioned as Flagship of the Pacific Fleet.
1893	29 August. Commissioned as Queenstown Flagship.
1899	28 March. Commissioned at Chatham for Pacific.
1902	January. Paid off at Chatham.
1905	4 April. Sold to Ward of Preston.

RODNEY 'Admiral' class barbette.

10,300 tons; 330' x 68½' x 27½'; 17½ knots; complement 530;
Armament 13.5" BL, 6 x 6" BL, 12 x 6 pdr QF, 10 x 3 pdr QF, 5 x 14" TT.

Laid down 6 February, 1882; launched 8 October, 1884.
A particularly successful class of battleship, the 'Admirals' were built to counter a dramatic growth in the size of the French navy. A low freeboard, however, meant that main guns were forever awash. Completed in June 1888, this unduly lengthy period resulted from delays in the manufacture of the *Rodney's* four 13.5" guns.

1888	20 June. Commissioned at Chatham and joined Home Fleet.
1890-94	Channel duties.
1894-97	Mediterranean.
1897-1901	Coastguard duties, Queensferry.
1901	March. Paid off at Chatham and joined Reserve.
1907	Laid up.
1909	11 May. Sold for scrap to Ward's of Morecambe.

MERSEY Name ship of class of twin screw second class cruiser.

4,050 tons; 300' x 46' x 19½'; 18 knots; complement 300.
Armament 2 x 8" BL, 10 x 6" BL, 3 x 6 pdr QF, 3 x 3 pdr QF, 4 x TT.

Laid down 9 July, 1883; launched 31 March, 1885.
First vessel built at Chatham to abandon any form of sailing rig.

1887	Completed. Remained at Chatham until 1893.
1893	9 May. Commissioned for Coastguard duties, Harwich.
1898	May. Paid off. Chatham.
1905	4 April. Sold to Isaacs.

SEVERN 'Mersey' class twin screw second class cruiser.

4,050 tons; 300' x 46' x 19½"; 18 knots; complement 300;
Armament 2 x 8" BL, 10 x 6" BL, 3 x 6 pdr QF, 3 x 3 pdr QF, 4 x TT.

Laid down 1 January, 1884; launched 29 September, 1885.

1888	Completed and sent to Portsmouth for commissioning.
1889	19 February. Commissioned for China station.
1895	June. Paid off.
1898	22 May. Commissioned at Chatham for Coastguard duties, Harwich.
1904	Paid off and retained at Chatham.
1905	4 April. Sold. G. Garnham.

HERO   'Conqueror' class turret ram battleship.

6,200 tons; 270′ x 58′ x 22′; 14 knots; complement 330;
Armament 2 x 12″ BL, 4 x 6″ BL, 7 x 6 pdr QF.

Laid down 11 April, 1884; undocked 27 October, 1885.
First vessel built at Chatham to abandon any form of sailing rig.
1888   May. Completed at Chatham, and then dispatced to Portsmouth for
           commissioning.
1888-1904 Tender to the naval gunnery school *Excellent*.
1905   February. Relegated to dockyard Reserve.
1907   November. Became a target ship.
1908   18 February. Sunk off Kentish Knock.

IMMORTALITE   'Orlando' class twin screw second class cruiser.

5,600 tons; 300′ x 56′ x 22½′; 18 knots; complement 484;
Armament 2 x 9.2″ BL, 10 x 6″ BL, 10 x 3 pdr QF, 6 x 6 pdr QF, 6 x 18″ TT.
An enlarged *Mersey*, the *Immortalite* was designed for trade protection.

Laid down 18 January, 1886; undocked 7 June, 1887.
1890   1 July. Commissioned at Chatham for Channel squadron.
1895   April. Paid off at Chatham.
           19 November. Commissioned at Chatham for China station.
1899   October. Paid off at Sheerness.
1901   May. Commissioned at Sheerness as tender to *Wildfire* for gunnery
           duty.
1905   April. Paid off at Sheerness then laid up in Holy Loch.
1907   Sold for breaking up.

MEDEA   'Magicienne' class twin screw second class cruiser.

2,800 tons; 265′ x 41′ x 16½′; 20 knots; complement 218;
Armament 6 x 6″ BL, 9 x 6 pdr QF, 1 x 3 pdr QF, 2 x 18″ TT.

Laid down 25 April, 1887; launched 9 June, 1888.
Similar to the *Mersey*, but smaller. Generally considered rather inferior.
Eventually reduced to third class cruiser status.
1895   April. Fitting out at Chatham completed.
           12 November. Commissioned as drill ship. Removed to Southampton.
1901   Paid off and possibly refitted at Jarrow.
1902   8 October. Commissioned at Jarrow for 'Particular Service'.
1904   Laid up at Sheerness.
1905   Laid up. River Blackwater.
1908   Laid up. Portsmouth.
1909   27 April. Commissioned at Chatham for Mediterranean.
1914   2 April. Sold.

MEDUSA   'Magicienne' class twin screw second class cruiser.

2,800 tons; 265' x 41' x 16½'; 20 knots; complement 218;
Armament 6 x 6" BL, 9 x 6 pdr QF, 1 x 3 pdr QF, 2 x 18" TT.

Laid down 25 August, 1887; launched 11 August, 1888.
1895   Fitting out at Chatham completed.
          12 November. Commissioned as drill ship. Removed to South Shields.
1901   Paid off and possibly refitted at Jarrow.
1902   10 April. Commissioned at Jarrow for Cruiser Training squadron.
1904   3 May. Commissioned at Devonport as tender to the training ship *Impregnable.*
1905   Laid up at Motherbank.
1908   January. Transferred to Sheerness and placed on sale list.
1909   October. Refitting at Pembroke dock.
1910   August. Towed to Bantry Bay for use as calibrating vessel.
1917-18 Harbour service at Queenstown.
1920   Sold to Stanlee of Dover and then resold to J.E. Thomas in 1921.

RESEARCH   Paddle survey vessel.

520 tons; 155' x 24' x 8½'; 10½ knots; complement 80;
Armament 1 x 6 pdr QF.

Laid down 13 September, 1887; launched 4 December, 1888.
Constructed in the No. 5 slip, *Research* was the first paddle wheel steamer built in the yard for over twenty years. Purpose built for surveying the West coast, she had an exceptionally shallow draught.
1887   5 November. Originally laid down as *Investigator,* but re-named.
1889   24 April. Commissioned at Chatham.
1915   Depot ship at Portland.
1920   July. Sold to Ward, New Holland.

SHELDRAKE   'Sharpshooter' class twin screw first class torpedo gunboat.

735 tons; 230' x 27' x 10'; 21 knots; complement 91;
Armament 2 x 4.7" QF, 4 x 3 pdr QF, 3 x 14" TT.

Laid down 4 July, 1888; launched 30 March, 1889.
First torpedo gun boat to be built in Chatham dockyard.
1894   Commissioned at Chatham for coast guard duties, Hull.
1898   Paid off. Devonport.
1902   Tender to *Pembroke.*
1905   Laid up at Chatham.
1905-07 Laid up. Forth.
1907   July. Sold.

SKIPJACK   'Sharpshooter' class twin screw first class torpedo gunboat.

735 tons; 230' x 27' x 10'; 21 knots; complement 91;
Armament 2 x 4.7" QF, 4 x 3 pdr QF, 3 x 14" TT.

Laid down 4 July, 1888; launched 30 April, 1889.
1894   16 January. Commissioned at Chatham for Mediterranean.
1898   Paid off at Chatham by this date.
1904   Tender to Drillship, Queenstown.
1905   Coastguard duties and later fishery protection duties.
1909   Fitted with sweeps.
1914   Joined Grand Fleet as a minesweeper.
1916   With 2nd Minesweeper Flotilla and in 1918 joined 13th Flotilla.
1920   April. Sold to Hammond Lane Foundry Company, for breaking up.

SALAMANDER   'Sharpshooter' class twin screw first class torpedo gunboat.

735 tons; 230' x 27' x 10'; 21 knots; complement 91;
Armament 2 x 4.7" QF, 4 x 3 pdr QF, 3 x 14" TT.

Laid down 23 April, 1888; launched 31 May, 1889.
1894   Commissioned for coastguard duties, Portland.
1898   15 September. Commissioned at Devonport for Mediterranean.
1901   Paid off at Devonport by this date.
1906   15 May. Sold to Ashdown.

SEAGULL   'Sharpshooter' class twin screw first class torpedo gunboat.

735 tons; 230' x 27' x 10'; 21 knots; complement 91;
Armament 2 x 4.7" QF, 4 x 3 pdr QF, 3 x 14" TT.

Laid down 23 April, 1888; launched 31 May, 1889.
1890   At Portsmouth. Tender to *Vernon* until 1895.
1898   Portsmouth Reserve.
1899   Commissioned at Portsmouth as tender to depot ship *Duke of
          Wellington* and, from 1904, *Firequeen.*
1905-08   Tender to *Victory.*
1909   Fitted with sweeps and joined the Home Fleet as a minesweeper.
1914   August. Joined Grand Fleet.
1915-18   Transferred to Lowestoft (1915), Harwich (1915) and then Oban
          (1917).
1918   30 September. Sunk in Firth of Forth as the result of a collision.

HMS BLAKE (1889)

BLAKE Name ship of class of twin screw first class cruiser.

9,150 tons; 375' x 65' x 24'; 22 knots; complement 570;
Armament 2 x 9.2" BL, 10 x 6" QF, 16 x 3 pdr QF, 4 x 14" TT.

Laid down July, 1888; launched 23 November, 1889.
The largest cruiser built up to that point in time, the *Blake* was designed for long range trade protection.

1892	Commissioned at Chatham as flagship of the North American and West Indies station.
1895	December. Commissioned for Channel squadron after being paid off at Chatham in June of this same year.
1898	6 December. Paid off at Devonport.
1900	30 October. Commissioned at Devonport for trooping to the Mediterranean.
1901	15 July. Paid off and entered Devonport Reserve.
1907	Converted to Depot ship, joining Home Fleet destroyers of Nore Division in January 1908.
1910-21	Continued in service as a depot ship, eventually ending up in the Harwich Reserve Fleet.
1921	13 October. Paid off into Nore Reserve.
1922	9 June. Sold to Rees of Llanelly.

ANDROMACHE   'Apollo' class twin screw second class cruiser.

3,400 tons; 300' x 44' x 17½'; 20 knots; complement 273;
Armament 2 x 6" QF, 6 x 4.7" QF, 8 x 6 pdr QF, 1 x 3 pdr QF, 4 x 14" TT.

Laid down April, 1889; launched 14 August, 1890.

1892-99	Not in general commission. Held at Chatham, but made appearances during various annual manoeuvres held during those years.
1901	1 July. Commissioned at Devonport for Royal Naval Reserve drillship duties at North Shields.
1904	Royal Naval Reserve drillship at Harwich.
1905	Returned to Chatham and laid up.
1905-08	Laid up, River Blackwater.
1908	November. Returned to Chatham so that work could begin on converting her to that of a minelayer. Most of her armament was removed together with upper and main deck partitions. Eventually she was given the capacity to store 100 mines on special trackways.
1909	September. Conversion to minelayer completed. Commissioned at Chatham for Home Fleet.
1910	Placed in Reserve at Nore joining the 2nd Fleet Reserve (Nore) in 1913.
1914	August. Acting as a Home Fleet minelayer, and based at Dover.
1915	January. Held at Chatham for repairs.
1916	Accommodation ship, Gibraltar.
1920	August. Purchased by S. Castle of Plymouth and broken up.

APOLLO   Name ship of class of twin screw second class cruisers.

3,400 tons; 300' x 44' x 17½'; 20 knots; complement 273;
Armament (1892) 2 x 6" QF, 6 x 4.7" QF, 8 x 6 pdr QF, 1 x 3 pdr QF 4 x 14" TT.
(1909) 4 x 4.7" QF, 100 mines.

Laid down April, 1889; launched 10 February, 1891.

1892-99	Not in general commission. Held at Chatham, but made appearances during various annual manoeuvres held during those years.
1901	1 July. Commissioned at Devonport as a Royal Naval Reserve drillship and placed at Southampton.
1905-08	Laid up at Portsmouth.
1908	Transferred to Chatham so that work could begin on her conversion to mine layer.
1909	4 August. Commissioned at Chatham for Home Fleet.
1910	Devonport Reserve Division.
1912	Transferred to 2nd Fleet Reserve.
1914	August. Acting as Home Fleet minelayer, and based at Dover. Transferred to Sheerness in 1915.
1915	October. Returned to Chatham dockyard for refit and then joined Nore Command.
1917	Depot ship. Devonport.
1920	2 February. Paid off at Devonport and sold to S. Castle of Plymouth for breaking up.

HMS APOLLO (1891)

HAWKE   'Edgar' class twin screw first class cruiser.

7,350 tons; 360' x 60¾' x 24'; 19½ knots; complement 540;
Armament 2 x 9.2" BL, 10 x 6" QF, 12 x 6 pdr QF, 4 x 18" TT.
Similar to *Blake,* but smaller with a reduced armoured deck. Considerable
endurance as the *Hawke* could carry sufficient coal for steaming 10,000 miles.

Laid down 17 June, 1889; launched 11 March, 1891.

1893	16 May. Commissioned at Chatham for Mediterranean.
1897	Engaged in operations that led to the pacification of Crete and the appointment of Prince George of Greece as High Commissioner. Included embarkation of Greek military force in Platania Bay.
1899	July. Paid off at Chatham and entered Reserve.
1902	1 April. Commissioned at Chatham for Special Service.
1903	Paid off in March, but recommissioned for Home Fleet in May.
1904	Paid off in May and recommissioned for training service in November.
1905	Fourth Cruiser Squadron, West Indies.
1906	In Reserve at Chatham, becoming Sheerness Torpedo School tender in November.
1907	16 November. Commissioned for Nore Reserve of Home Fleet.
1908	Portsmouth Reserve Division.
1911	20 September. Whilst in Solent, collided with the White Star liner, *Olympic. Hawke* lost her ram, this being later replaced by a straight bow. Theories at the time suggested the cruiser had been sucked in towards the larger vessel. No blame attributed.
1913	4 February. Commissioned at Portsmouth for Training Squadron based at Queenstown.
1914	August. With 10th Cruiser Squadron of the 3rd Fleet.
	15 October. Whilst patrolling in the North Sea, *Hawke* was sunk by the U-9. Only 31 officers and men survived.

HMS HAWKE showing damage after collision with Olympic

HMS HOOD (1891)

HOOD   **'Royal Sovereign' class battleship.**

14,150 tons; 380′ x 75′ x 27½′; 15½ knots; complement 690;
Armament 4 x 13.5″ BL 10 x 6″ QF, 12 x 6 pdr QF, 12 x 3 pdr QF, 5 x 18″ TT.

Laid down 12 August, 1889; launched 30 June, 1891.
Built as a turret ship, the *Hood* was the last first class battleship to incorporate
such a design.

1893	1 June. Commissioned at Chatham for Mediterranean.
1900	29 April. Paid off for a refit at Chatham.
	12 December. Commissioned at Chatham for Mediterranean.
1902-03	Returned to Chatham for a long refit.
1903	25 June. Commissioned at Devonport for Home Fleet.
1904	28 September. Paid off at Devonport and entered Reserve.
1906	21 April. Commissioned at Chatham for Devonport Reserve Division of Home Fleet.
1910	July. Receiving ship at Queenstown but later became a receiving ship at Devonport.
1911	Employed as a target for underwater protection experiments and was first ship to be fitted with a bulge.
1914	August. By this date, she had been placed on sale list, but her name was consequently removed.
	4 November. Converted to blockship, and sunk at the southern entrance of Portland Harbour.

BARFLEUR   'Centurion' class battleship.

10,500 tons; 360′ x 70′ x 25′; 17 knots; complement 620;
Armament 4 x 10″ BL, 10 x 4.7″ QF, 8 x 6 pdr QF, 12 x 3 pdr QF, 7 x 18″ TT.

Laid down 12 October, 1890; launched 10 August, 1892.
A more lightly armed battleship designed specifically for service on foreign stations. The comparatively shallow draught allowed passage through the Suez Canal.

1895	26 February. Commissioned at Chatham for Mediterranean, relieving the *Sans Pareil*.
1898	September. Transferred to China station. Her white paint, an obligatory feature of service on this station, having a distinct bluish hue, earned her the title 'Far bluer'.
1900	Participated in landing operations conducted at the time of the Boxer uprising. Amongst members of the crew injured during fighting around Tientsin was the future Admiral of the Fleet, Earl Beatty. He was serving as Commander in the *Barfleur* at the time.
1902	Paid off at Devonport and entered Reserve.
	August. Major refit at Devonport. Work completed July 1904.
1904	5 August. During annual manoeurvres collided with *Canopus* whilst in Mounts Bay.
1905	Commissioned at Devonport for trooping to Mediterranean.
	Took out crew of *Vengeance.*
	May. Flagship of Portsmouth Reserve Fleet.
1909	April. Joined 4th Division of Home Fleet but, in June, laid up at Motherbank.
1910	12 July. Sold to Ewen of Glasgow.

HMS BARFLEUR (1894)

DRYAD   Name ship of class of torpedo gunboats.

1,070 tons; 250' x 30½' x 11½'; 18 knots; complement 120;
Armament 2 x 4.7" QF, 4 x 6 pdr QF, 5 x 18" TT.

Laid down 15 April, 1893; undocked 22 November, 1893.

1895	17 January. Commissioned at Chatham for Mediterranean, returning to Chatham in 1898.
1899	Commissioned at Chatham for Mediterranean, transferring to East Indies July 1902.
1904	Paid off at Malta.
1905	January. At Harwich, acting as tender to *Scylla*.
1906	30 January. Commissioned at Chatham as tender to Portsmouth navigation school.
1914	August. Operating at Lerwick as part of 10th Cruiser Squadron.
1915	Conversion to minesweeper and based at Lowestoft.
1918	January. Re-named *Hamadryad* and placed on harbour service.
1920	24 September. Sold to H. Auten for breaking up.

FORTE   'Astraea' class twin screw second class cruiser.

4,360 tons; 320' x 49½' x 19'; 19¾ knots; complement 318;
Armament 2 x 6" QF, 8 x 4.7" QF, 8 x 6 pdr QF, 1 x 3 pdr QF, 4 x 18" TT.
An improved 'Apollo' with better sea keeping qualities.

Laid down 21 September, 1891; launched 9 December, 1893.

1895	5 November. Commissioned at Chatham for Mediterranean. Detached Cape, January to March 1897. Activities at this time included participation in the Benin expedition under Rear-Admiral H.H. Rawson. The object of this being to capture Benin after officers of the Niger Coast Protectorate were massacred.
1898	16 October. Paid off at Chatham.
1899	Commissioned at Chatham for Cape and West Coast of Africa, participating in Second Boer War. Contributed to naval brigade which assisted in the relief of Ladysmith. The ship, herself, helped blockade Delagoa Bay.
1906	Portsmouth Reserve.
1909	20 April. Commissioned at Portsmouth for Cape station.
1913	June. Paid off at Chatham and entered Reserve.
	July. Laid up at Kethole Reach, River Medway.
1914	2 April. Sold.

HMS FORTE (1893)

MAGNIFICENT   'Majestic' class battleship.

14,900 tons; 390′ x 75′ x 26½′; 19¾ knots; complement 318;
Armament 4 x 12″ BL, 12 x 6″ QF, 18 x 12 pdr QF, 12 x 3 pdr QF, 5 x 18″ TT.

Laid down 8 December, 1893; undocked 19 December, 1894.
A much improved design over previous battleships, a particular feature of the
'Majestic' class, of which three were built at Chatham, was its main armament
of four 12″ guns of a new type that had a high rate of fire combined with
greater penetration.

1895	12 December. Commissioned at Chatham for Channel Squadron.
1904	2 February. Paid off Devonport for refit.
	16 July. Commissioned at Devonport for Channel Squadron but transferred in December to Atlantic.
1905	14 June. Explosion in main gun turret, 18 casualties.
1906	6 November. Commissioned at Chatham for Nore Reserve and attached to Sheerness gunnery school.
1907	Major refit at Chatham dockyard that included conversion to oil fuel. *Magnificent* was one of the first large ships to use oil being provided with a 400 ton capacity together with her normal load of 900 tons of coal. Fire control also fitted at this time.
1908	August. Commissioned as second flagship to Home Fleet.
1909	Chatham Reserve Division before recommissioning as flagship to Nore Reserve Division.
1910	3 December. Slightly damaged after collision with SS *Veratyr* at Sheerness.
1912	May. Transferred to Devonport and became a sea going naval gunnery training ship. Whilst in this role she ran aground in fog near Cawsand Pier (16 June 1913) sustaining slight damage.
1913	1 July. Entered Devonport Reserve.
1914	August. Commissioned for 9th Battle Squadron based on Grimsby.
1915	January. Transferred to Scapa. At this point it had been decided to remove her main 12″ guns for use by 'Lord Clive' class monitors. Subsequently, therefore, reduced to trooping and accommodation ship status.
1918	January. Fitting out at Belfast as ammunition storeship.
	November. Based at Rosyth.
1921	May. Sold to Ward of Inverkeithing.

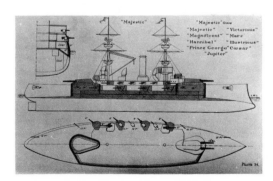

MAJESTIC CLASS,

MAGNIFICENT (1894),

VICTORIOUS (1895),

ILLUSTRIOUS (1896)

MINERVA   'Eclipse' class twin screw secnd class cruiser.

5,600 tons; 350′ x 54′ x 20½′; 18½ knots; complement 450;
Armament (1897) 5 x 6″ QF, 6 x 4.7″ QF, 8 x 12 pdr QF, 6 x 3 pdr QF, 3 x 18″ TT.
(1904) 11 x 6″, 8 x 12 pdr QF, 3 x 18″ TT.

Laid down 4 December, 1893; launched 23 September, 1895.
First Chatham cruiser to be fitted with a fighting top.

1897	4 February. Commissioned for 'Particular Service'.
	August. Paid off at Chatham.
1899	31 October. Commissioned at Chatham for Training Squadron.
1903	11 November. Paid off at Devonport and rearmed.
1904	9 June. Commissioned at Devonport for Mediterranean. Remained on this station (except for a refit at Chatham in 1908) until 1912 when she was paid off into 3rd Fleet (Reserve).
1912	August. Temporary depot ship.
1913	29 August. Paid off at Portsmouth.
1914	Later transferred to Egyptian waters and, in 1917, East Africa.
1918	Placed on Cape station.
1920	5 October. Sold to H. Auten for breaking up.

HMS MINERVA (1895)

VICTORIOUS   'Majestic' class battleship.

14,900 tons; 390' x 75' x 26½'; 19¾ knots; complement 318;
Armament 4 x 12" BL, 12 x 6" QF, 18 x 12 pdr QF, 12 x 3 pdr QF, 5 x 18" TT.

Laid down 28 May, 1894; launched 19 October, 1895.
As with others of the 'Majestic' class, the Victorious was amongst the oldest
of battleships to see service during World War One.

1897	8 June. Commissioned for Channel Fleet, but transferred to Mediterranean in January of the following year.
1898	February. Ordered to China but grounded (14.2.1898) near Port Said. Refloated and left for China.
1900	16 May. Recommissioned at Malta for Mediterranean.
1903	8 August. Returned to Chatham for paying off and refit.
1904	February. Rear-Admiral's flagship, Channel and later transferred to Atlantic.
	14 July. Rammed by TB 113 whilst in Hamoaze. Sustained damage to side plating.
1905	Returned to Devonport and recommissioned for Nore Reserve Division. Subsequently commissioned at Chatham in April 1909 and May 1910 for the same service.
1909	March. Dry docked for refit, during which she received provisions for oil storage together with a fire control system.
1910	5 June. Internal explosion through spontaneous ignition of coal.
1911	January. Transferred to Devonport Division Home Fleet and, in August of that year, entered 3rd Reserve Fleet.
1912	14 July. Collided with Majestic during manoeuvres. Damage restricted to starboard engine and sternwalk.
1913	December. Refit at Devonport.
1914	August. With 9th Battle Squadron based on Grimsby. Clearly, however, obsolete.
1915	1 January. Decision taken to remove armament for use on new Monitor designs.
	February. Arrival at Elswick so that her 12" guns could be removed and transferred to Prince Rupert and General Wolfe.
1916	March. Became a repair ship.
1920	Re-named Indus II.
1922	19 December. Sold to A.J. Purves and later re-sold to Stanlee of Dover for breaking up.

ILLUSTRIOUS   'Majestic' class battleship.

14,900 tons; 390' x 75' x 26½'; 19¾ knots; complement 318;
Armament 4 x 12" BL, 12 x 6" QF, 18 x 12 pdr QF, 12 x 3 pdr, 5 x 18" TT.

Laid down 11 March, 1895; launched 17 September, 1896.

1898	10 May. Commissioned at Chatham for Mediterranean. First tour of duty included operations off Crete during the insurrection of late 1898. Remained in Mediterranean until 1904.
1904	July. Commissioned for Channel, later transferred to Atlantic.
1905	14 September. Paid off at Chatham and underwent a short refit.
1906	24 March. Commissioned at Chatham for Nore Reserve.
	3 April. Recommissioned for Channel Fleet.
1908	2 June. Returned to Chatham and then commissioned for Portsmouth Reserve Division.
1912	15 June. Commissioned at Devonport for 3rd Fleet Devonport.
1914	August. With 7th Battle Squadron at Devonport. Later became guardship at Loch Ewe.
1915	January. Decision taken to remove her main 12" guns for use by 'Lord Clive' class monitors. This work subsequently undertaken.
1916	Having been converted to ammunition storeship, the *Illustrious* was temporarily based on the Tyne.
1917	Transferred to Portsmouth for same duties. Remained until 1919.
1920	18 June. Sold to Ward of Barrow.

VINDICTIVE   'Arrogant' class twin screw second class cruiser.

5,750 tons; 320' x 57½' x 21'; 19 knots; complement 480;
Armament 4 x 6" QF, 6 x 4.7" QF, 8 x 12 pdr QF, 3 x 3 pdr QF, 2 x 18" TT.
(In 1904 all 6" and 4.7" guns were removed and replaced by 10 x 6" QFs.)

Laid down 27 January, 1896; undocked 9 December, 1897.
Designed for operating with the fleet, the *Vindictive* was also armed with an underwater ram.

1900   4 July. Commissioned at Chatham for Mediterranean.
1904   8 February. Paid off at Chatham and entered Reserve remaining there, except for a brief spell of trooping in 1906, until 1911.
1912   15 March. Recommissioned at Portsmouth as tender to *Vernon*.
1914   August. With 9th Cruiser squadron.
1915   East Coast of South America, before transfer to White Sea in 1916.
1918   February. Fitting out at Chatham as an assault ship.
        10 May. Sunk as a blockship at Ostende, but subsequently raised and broken up in 1920.

The last rôle for the VINDICTIVE — sunk as a blockship at Ostend, ship was raised again by the British in 1920.

44

HMS VINDICTIVE (1897)

GOLIATH   'Canopus' first class battleship.

12,950 tons; 390' x 74' x 25'; 18¼ knots; complement 682;
Armament 4 x 12" BL, 12 x 6" QF, 12 x 12 pdr QF, 6 x 1 pdr QF, 5 x 18" TT.

Laid down 4 January, 1897; launched 23 March, 1898.
Designed to operate on the China station, acting as a counter weight to
Japanese Fleet expansion, the *Goliath* had a draught sufficiently shallow to
allow her to use the Suez Canal.

1900	27 March. Commissioned at Chatham for China station playing, in that year, a small part in the Boxer uprising.
1901	September. Refitting at Hong Kong before returning to active duty in April of the following year.
1904	Jan-July. Refit at Palmers, U.K.
1905	With Mediterranean Fleet from May, but transferred to Channel in December.
1907-08	Refit to machinery and fire control added.
1908	October. During passage to Malta, damaged her propeller shaft, being retained in that dockyard for a further refit. Repairs completed, January 1909.
1909	April. Commissioned at Sheerness for Nore Reserve.
1911	Refitting at Chatham prior to joining the Pembroke Reserve.
1914	August. With the 8th Battle squadron operating out of Devonport. Later transferred to Loch Ewe for defence of Grant Fleet anchorage. September. Dispatched to East Indies for escort duties. November. Operated against the German light cruiser *Konigsberg.*
1915	April. Transferred to Dardanelles, in order to support landings upon the beaches around Cape Helles. On May 13 she was sunk by the Turkish torpedo boat *Muavenet* which was, at that time, manned by a German crew. Of the *Goliath's* crew, 570 were killed.

HMS GOLIATH (1898)

IRRESISTIBLE   'Formidable' class first class battleship.

15,000 tons; 430' x 75' x 27'; 18½ knots; complement 780;
Armament 4 x 12" BL, 12 x 6" QF, 16 x 12 pdr QF, 6 x 3 pdr QF, 6 x 18" TT.

Laid down 11 April, 1898; launched 15 December, 1898.
Larger than any previous battleship built at Chatham, the *Irresistible* not only
mounted 12" guns of an increased calibre, but also had a larger number of
12-pdrs. Engine horse power was much improved, with a consequent increase
of speed.

1902	4 February. Commissioned at Chatham for Mediterranean.
	3 March. Whilst proceeding to her new station the *Goliath* collided with the *SS Clive*. Sustaining considerable damage, emergency repairs were immediately required.
1904	30 November. Returned to Chatham for paying off. Limited refit prior to recommissioning for Mediterranean in December.
1905	9 October. Grounded off Malta.
1908	January. Transferred to Channel Fleet.
	4 May. Collided with schooner in heavy fog. Nothing more than superficial damage sustained on this occasion.
	15 December. Commissioned at Chatham for Reserve.
1910-11	Seven month refit undertaken at Chatham dockyard.
1913	27 March. Recommissioned at Portsmouth for 2nd Fleet (Reserve).
1914	August. With 5th Battle squadron on Channel patrol.
1915	January. Ordered to Eastern Mediterranean for purposes of joining the naval expedition then being prepared for the bombardment of the Gallipoli Peninsula.
	18 March. In company with a large Anglo-French Fleet, the *Irresistible* entered the Dardanelles, opening fire on various Turkish fortifications. At approximately 4.15 however, she came too close in shore and struck one of twenty recently laid Turkish mines. Completely disabled she drifted further in-shore and was eventually sunk by enemy gun fire.

HMS IRRESISTIBLE (1898) undergoing completion work in the fitting out basin at Chatham.

PIONEER 'Pelorous' class twin screw third class cruiser.

2,200 tons; 305' x 36½' x 16'; 20 knots; complement 224;
Armament 8 x 4", 8 x 3 pdr QF, 2 x 14" TT.

Laid down 16 December, 1897; undocked 28 June, 1899.
In order to obtain greater speed, *Pioneer* was designed with a long narrow hull
and fitted with a new style Thorneycroft water tube boiler.

1900	15 November. Commissioned at Chatham for Mediterranean.
1905	3 January. Reduced to Reserve after returning to Chatham.
	July. Transferred to Australia station as a drill ship.
1910	5 January. Rescued crew of *Walkare,* an American ship wrecked off New Zealand.
1912	1 July. Transferred to Royal Australian Navy.
	30 November. Paid off at Sydney.
1913	1 March. Presented to the Australian navy as a gift from the British Admiralty.
1914	1 January. Commissioned at Sydney for training duties.
	4 August. At the outbreak of war the *Pioneer* was moored in Port Philip, being ordered to patrol the coastline of Western Australia.
	16 August. Captured the German merchant vessel *Neumunster.*
	26 August. Captured the German merchant vessel *Thuringen.*
	3 November. Damaged in heavy seas. Returned to Fremantle for repairs.
1915	January. Ordered to East Coast of Africa in order to strengthen naval operations directed towards the eventual capture of German colonies.
	February. Joined other units engaged in blockading the *Konigsberg.* Since September this German light cruiser had been trapped in the Rufigi River, but protected by mangrove swamps that prevented a closer approach.
1916	18 March. Destroyed German supply ship *Tabora* whilst patrolling Indian ocean.
	13 June. Bombarded Dar-Es-Salaam, then capital of German East Africa.
	8 August. Ordered to return to Australia.
	22 August. Sailed from Zamzibar flying Pay-off pennant.
	November. Paid off at Sydney and entered Reserve as an accommodation ship. Saw no further war service and was eventually sold in 1926.
1931	18 February. Hull scuttled off Sydney Heads.

VENERABLE   'London' class first class battleship.

15,000 tons; 400' x 75' x 29'; 18 knots; complement 740;
Armament 4 x 12", 12 x 6" QF, 16 x 12 pdr QF, 6 x 3 pdr QF, 4 x 18" TT.

Laid down 2 January, 1899; launched 2 November, 1899.
Little difference externally from *Irresistible* but the *Venerable* had a longer belt of armour amidships.

1902	12 December. Commissioned at Chatham as second Flagship to the Mediterranean Fleet.
1905	26 June. Scraped keel on bottom of Algiers harbour, sustaining slight damage.
1909	6 January. Paid off at Chatham, later entering dry dock for a major refit.
	19 October. Commissioned at Chatham for Atlantic Fleet.
1912	May. Transferred to 5th Battle squadron (Reserve).
1914	August. Allocated to Vice-Admiral, Dover, for bombardment duties of Belgian coast.
1915	March. Bombarded Westende batteries.
	May. Ordered to Dardanelles. Later attached to Italian Fleet. Spent much of the rest of the war held in Reserve at Taranto harbour. Partially disarmed and used as a depot ship.
1918	January. Paid off at Portsmouth.
	November. Depot ship at Granton.
1920	4 June. Sold for breaking up. Eventually taken to Germany.

ALBEMARLE   'Duncan' class first class battleship.

14,000 tons; 405' x 75' x 25'; 19 knots; complement 780;
Armament 4 x 12", 12 x 6" QF, 12 x 12 pdr QF, 6 x 3 pdr QF, 4 x 18" TT.

Laid down 8 January, 1900; launched 5 March, 1901.
A smaller and faster version of the *Venerable*.

1903	12 November. Commissioned at Chatham for Mediterranean.
1905	January. Transferred to Channel Fleet.
1907	February. Second Flagship to Atlantic Fleet. Collided with *Commonwealth* (11 February), receiving only slight damage.
1910	Portsmouth Reserve Division.
1913	Gunnery training duties, Portsmouth.
1914	August. Joined 3rd Battle squadron of Grand Fleet and employed on northern patrols.
1915	February. Joined the 6th Battle squadron of the Channel Fleet but later tranferred to the 3rd Battle squadron.
	November. Whilst heavily laden with ammunition she met heavy weather in the Pentland Firth. Bridge completely washed away and immediate repairs were necessitated.
1916	January. Transferred to Archangel as an ice breaker and guardship.
	September. Recalled for refit.
1917	May. Overflow ship, naval barracks, Devonport.
1919	19 November. Sold to Cohen of Swansea for breaking up.

HMS ALBEMARLE (1901)

PRINCE OF WALES   'London' class first class battleship.

15,000 tons; 400' x 75' x 29'; 18 knots; complement 750;
Armament 4 x 12", 12 x 6" QF, 16 x 12 pdr QF, 6 x 3 pdr QF, 4 x 18" TT.

Laid down 2 January, 1899; launched 25 March, 1902.
Last of the pre-Dreadnoughts to mount a secondary armament of 12 x 6" guns.

1904	18 May. Commissioned at Chatham for Mediterranean.
1905	29 July. Collided with *SS Endiween* whilst off the coast of Algeria.
1906	28 May. Paid off at Portsmouth and entered Reserve.
	June-November. Refit. ·
	September. Commissioned at Portsmouth for Mediterranean.
1908	November. Transferred to Atlantic Fleet. Flagship of Commander-in-Chief.
1909	2 July. Internal explosion close to engine room but sustained only slight damage.
1911	February-May. Refit. Gibraltar.
1912	May. Transferred to 3rd Battle squadron.
1913	Portsmouth Reserve Division.
	2 June. During that year's naval exercise collided with submarine C.32.
1914	August. 5th Battle Squadron operating in the Channel.
1915	March. Transferred to Dardanelles and employed upon coastal bombardment duties.
1917	January. Officially attached to Italian Fleet.
1918	January. Returned to Portsmouth, service as an accommodation ship.
1920	12 April. Sold to Ward's of Milford Haven and broken up.

The battleship PRINCE OF WALES under construction in 1901.

HMS CHALLENGER (1902)

CHALLENGER   Name ship of class of twin screw second class cruisers.

5,880 tons; 355' x 54' x 20½'; 21 knots; complement 450;
Armament 11 x 6" QF, 9 x 12 pdr QF, 6 x 3 pdr QF, 2 x 18" TT.

Laid down 1 December, 1900; undocked 27 May, 1902.
1904   3 May. Commissioned at Chatham for Australia, serving with the
          Imperial squadron on the Australia station from November.
          31 October. Paid off at Devonport for refit.
1914   August. 9th Cruiser squadron operating out of Portland.
1915   Transferred to East Africa, operating off Dar-Es-Salaam.
          July. Participated in destruction of *Konigsberg*.
1916   13 June. In company with HMAS *Pioneer* bombarded Dar-Es-
          Salaam, capital of German East Africa.
1919   1 April. Paid off at Portsmouth.
1920   31 May. Sold to Ward of Preston for breaking up.

HMS DEVONSHIRE (1904)

DEVONSHIRE   Name ship of class of twin screw first class cruiser.

10,850 tons; 450' x 68½' x 24'; 22 knots; complement 655;
Armament 4 x 7.5", 6 x 6" QF, 2 x 12 pdr QF, 18 x 3 pdr QF, 2 x 18" TT.

Laid down 25 March, 1902; launched 30 April, 1904.

1905	24 March. Commissioned at Chatham and entered Reserve.
	24 October. Commissioned at Chatham for 1st Cruiser squadron, Home Fleet.
1907	March. Commissioned at Chatham for 2nd Cruiser squadron, Home Fleet.
1909	19 March. Reduced to Devonport Reserve Division.
1913-16	3rd Cruiser squadron Home/Grand Fleet (detached October 1915).
1916-19	North American and West Indies station returning to Devonport in July, 1919.
1921	June. Sold for breaking up.

AFRICA   'King Edward VII' class first class battleship.

16,350 tons; 454′ x 78′ x 24½′; 19 knots; complement 777;
Armament 4 x 12″, 4 x 9,2″, 10 x 6″ QF, 12 x 12 pdr QF, 14 x 3 pdr QF, 4 x 18″ TT.

Laid down 27 January, 1904; launched 20 May, 1905.
For Chatham dockyard, *Africa* was an important ship for many reasons.
Amongst all else, however, it was both the last and largest battleship built
within the yard, also being the first ship launched from the No. 8 slip. A major
feature of this particular vessel was her intermediate 9.2″ armament.

1906	6 November. Commissioned at Chatham for the Atlantic Fleet.
1907	March. In collision with *SS Ormuz*.
1908	June. With 2nd Battle squadron of Home Fleet.
1912	January. Whilst at Sheerness Harbour she was fitted with a sloping seaplane runway that stretched forward from the bridge. From this, Flt-Lt Samson RN, made a successful take-off in a Short S.27.
1913	February. Attached to 3rd Battle squadron in the Mediterranean.
1914	August. Serving with 3rd Battle squadron of the Grand Fleet. Consisting of all eight 'King Edward VII' class battleships, the squadron was known as the 'Wobbly Eight'.
1915	Due to age, *Africa* withdrawn from active sea service and placed at the mouth of the Thames for purposes of countering the German battle cruiser threat.
1916-17	Serving in Mediterranean but later attached to 9th Cruiser squadron off West Africa.
1918	Entered Portsmouth for a refit before taking up duties as an accommodation ship.
1919	26 February. Paid off prior to being placed on sale list.
1920	June. Sold to Ellis of Newcastle.

HMS AFRICA (1905)

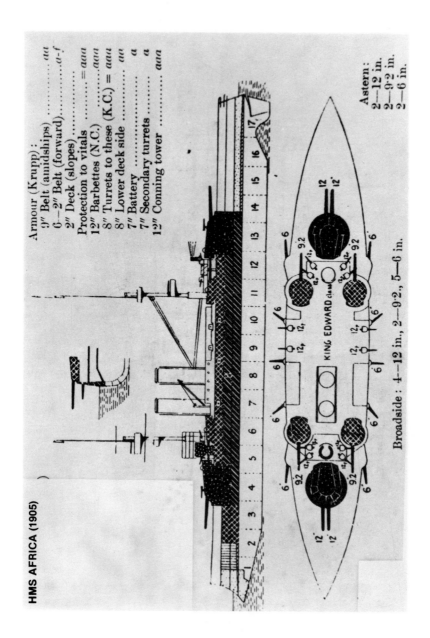

Armour (Krupp):
9" Belt (amidships) .... *aa*
6—2" Belt (forward) ....*a-f*
2" Deck (slopes) ....
Protection to vitals .... = *aaa*
12" Barbettes (N.C.) ....*aaa*
8" Turrets to these (K.C.) = *aaa*
8" Lower deck side .... *aa*
7" Battery .... *a*
7" Secondary turrets .... *a*
12" Conning tower .... *aaa*

Astern:
2—12 in.
2—9·2 in.
2—6 in.

Broadside: 4—12 in., 2—9·2., 5—6 in.

SHANNON 'Minotaur' class first class cruiser.

14,600 tons; 490′ x 75½′ x 26′; 22½ knots; complement 755;
Armament 4 x 9.2″, 10 x 7.5″, 16 x 12 pdr QF, 5 x 18″ TT.

Laid down 21 January, 1905; launched 20 September, 1906.
Generally considered a poor design, being under armoured.

1908	3 October. Commissioned at Chatham as Flagship to 5th Cruiser squadron of Home Fleet.
1909	April. 2nd Cruiser squadron of Home Fleet.
1912	3rd Cruiser squadron of Home Fleet.
1914-19	2nd Cruiser squadron, Grand Fleet.
1916	May. Present at the Battle of Jutland.
1917	12 December. Whilst patrolling convoy route between Lerwick and Norway, narrowly avoided engagement with *Admiral Scheer.*
1919	2 May. Paid off, becoming tender to *Actaeon,* the torpedo school at Sheerness.
1922	December. Sold to McLellan of Bo' Ness.

C.17 C-class submarine.

290 tons; 135′ x 13½′ x 12′; 13/8 knots; complement 16;
Armament 2 x 18″ TT.
Designed for coastal patrols, the C.17 was the first submarine ever to be built in a royal dockyard.

Laid down March, 1907; launched 13 August, 1908.

1909	Commissioned for 2nd (Submarine) Flotilla, Portsmouth.
1912	4th (Portsmouth) Flotilla.
1914	August. 4th (Dover) Flotilla.
1916	5th (Dover) Flotilla
1917-18	Returned to Chatham for a refit.
1918-19	Training duties, Clyde.
1919	November. Sold to J.A. Walker for breaking up.

HMS C17 (1908)

C. 18   C-class submarine

290 tons; 135' x 13½' x 12'; 13/8 knots; complement 16.
Armament 2 x 18" TT.

Laid down 1907; launched 10 September, 1908
1911   Commissioned for 2nd (Portsmouth) Flotilla for trials.
1912   Transferred to 4th (Portsmouth Flotilla.
1914   August. Operating with 4th (Dover) Flotilla and operated in Channel
            and Biscay areas until re-fit in 1915.
1916   With 5th (Dover) Flotilla.
1921   26 May. Sold to B. Fryer for breaking up.

C.19   C-class submarine.

290 tons; 135' x 13½' x 12'; 13/8 knots; complement 16;
Armament 2 x 18" TT.

Laid down 1 June, 1908; launched 20 March, 1909.
1909   Commissioned for 7th (Nore) Flotilla.
1914   7th (Tyne) Flotilla.
1914-15   10th (Humber) Flotilla.
1915   6th (Forth) Flotilla, later transferred to 7th Leith.
1916   5th (Dover) Flotilla.
1917-19   3rd (Humber) Flotilla.
1921   26 May. Sold to B. Fryer for breaking up.

C.20   C-class submarine.

290 tons; 135' x 13½' x 12'; 13/8 knots; complement 16;
Armament 2 x 18" TT.

Laid down 1 June, 1908; launched 27 November, 1909.
1910   Commissioned at Chatham for the 7th (Nore) Flotilla.
1914   August. Upon outbreak of war she was transferred to the 7th (Tyne)
            Flotilla, carrying out North Sea patrols.
1915   Transferred to the 6th (Forth) Flotilla before returning to the 7th
            Flotilla which had moved to Leith.
1916-17   6th (Portsmouth) Flotilla.
1917-18   1st (Portsmouth) Flotilla; 6th (Portsmouth) Flotilla.
1921   26 May. Sold to B. Fryer for breaking up.

C.33   C-class submarine.

290 tons; 135' x 13½' x 12'; 13/8 knots; complement 16;
Armament 2 x 18" TT.

Laid down March, 1909; launched 10 May, 1910.
1910   Commissioned at Chatham for 4th (Portsmouth) Flotilla.
1914   August. Upon outbreak of war transferred to 4th (Dover) Flotilla.
1915   4 August. Entered British minefield near Smith's Knoll, off Norfolk coast. Lost with entire crew.

C.34   C-class submarine.

290 tons; 135' x 13½' x 12'; 13/8 knots; complement 16;
Armament 2 x 18" TT.

Laid down March 1909; launched 8 June, 1910.
1910   Commissioned for 4th (Portsmouth) Flotilla.
1914   4th (Dover) Flotilla.
1916   6th (Portsmouth) Flotilla.
1917   21 July. Engaged in anti-submarine duties off the Shetlands. Was herself destroyed by U-52.

D.7   D-class submarine.

604 tons; 162' x 20½' x 14'; 16/9 knots; complement 25;
Armament 2 x 12 pdrs; 3 x 18" TT.

Laid down 1910; launched 14 January, 1911.
A much more advanced submarine than those of the 'C'-class, possessing a ⌐
diesel engine, twin screws, a W/T system and a gun mounting.

1911	Commissioned for 8th (Portsmouth) Flotilla.
1914-15	8th (Harwich) Flotilla.
1915-16	11th (Blyth) Flotilla.
1916-17	3rd (Immingham) Flotilla.
1917-18	'Platypus' Training Flotilla.
1918	6th (Portsmouth) Flotilla.
	February. Attacked by HMS *Pelican,* the look out having sited a periscope and assuming it to be that of a U-boat. Savagely depth charged, the D.7 was forced to the surface and then provided the crew of the destroyer with the necessary recognition signals.
1921	December. Sold to H. Pound for breaking up.

D.8   D-class submarine.

604 tons; 162' x 20½' x 14'; 16/9 knots; complement 25.
Armament 2 x 12 pdrs; 3 x 18" TT.

Laid down 1910; launched 23 September, 1911.

1911	Commissioned for 8th (Portsmouth) Flotilla.
1914	8th (Harwich) Flotilla.
	August. During Battle of Dogger Bank, D.8 was positioned at the mouth of the River Ems to torpedoe any returning German naval units.
1915-16	11th (Blyth) Flotilla.
1916-17	3rd (Immingham) Flotilla.
1917-18	'Platypus' Training Flotilla.
1921	December. Sold to H. Pound for breaking up.

HMS D8 (1911)

CHATHAM   Name ship of class of second class cruisers.

5,400 tons; 430' x 50' x 16'; 25½ knots; complement 400
Armament 8 x 6" QF, 1 x 3" AA, 2 x 21" TT.

Laid down 1910; launched 9 November, 1911.

1912	3 December. Commissioned at Chatham for 1st Light Cruiser Squadron, Home Fleet.
1914	August. Operating in Mediterranean under Admiral Sir Berkeley Milne. Involved in the pursuit of the German battle cruiser *Goeben* and the light cruiser *Breslau*. September. Detached to East Africa for purposes of locating the German light cruiser *Konigsberg*. In company with the *Dartmouth* and *Weymouth*, she located the enemy vessel hiding amongst the mangrove swamps of the Rufigi River. 10 November. Positioned and then sunk a converted collier at the mouth of the Rufigi, so preventing the *Konigsberg* making an easy escape.
1915	Returned to Mediterranean.
1916	May. Flagship of 3rd Light Cruiser Squadron (Home Fleet).
1919	July. Paid off to Nore Reserve.
1920	11 September. Commissioned at Chatham and loaned to the Royal New Zealand Navy to 1924.
1926	July. Held at Devonport. Placed on sale list and sold to Ward of Pembroke.

HMS CHATHAM (1911)

E.1　E-class submarine.

660 tons; 181' x 22½' x 12'; 16/10 knots; complement 30;
Armament 1 x 6 pdr; 4 x 18" TT.

Laid down 1912; launched 9 November, 1912.
Originally laid down as D.9.

1913	Commissioned at Chatham for 8th (Portsmouth) Flotilla.
1914	August. Transferred to Harwich.
	September. Plans finalised for the removal of E.1 (together with two further submarines) to the Baltic where she was to concentrate on attacking Russian shipping. For part of the mission she was under the command of Lt-Cdr Noel Laurence, senior officer to this small Baltic flotilla.
	October. Passed through Kattegat after leaving Gorleston on the 17th. Soon in action, firing two torpedoes upon the German cruiser *Victoria Luise*. Neither made contact.
1915	May. With the end of winter, the E.1 was again in action, patrolling the Bornholm area, and helping strangle Germany's vital iron-ore trade.
	19 August. Fired two torpedoes upon the battle cruiser *Moltke*, causing limited damage. The attack was sufficient to bring a sudden conclusion to German plans for a naval attack upon Riga.
1916	Continued to operate out of the Port of Reval on the Gulf of Finland throughout the summer period.
1917	Operational base moved from Reval to Helsinki in order to avoid affects of the constant upheaval then occurring on the Russian mainland. Even so, operations against the Germans had to cease.
1918	8 April. Under treaty of Brest-Litovsk all British submarines in the Baltic had to be surrendered to the Germans. Rather than accept this, the crews of various submarines, including the E.1, scuttled their respective vessels in the Gulf of Finland, just off Helsinki. The crews later returned to the UK via Archangel.

HMS E1 (1912)

E.2   E-class submarine.

660 tons; 181′ x 22½′ x 12′; 16/10 knots; complement 30;
Armament 1 x 6 pdr; 4 x 18″ TT.

Laid down 1912; launched 23 November, 1912.
Originally laid down as D.10

1913	Commissioned for 8th (Portsmouth) Flotilla.
1914	August. Transferred to Harwich for North Sea patrols.
1915	Despatched to Mediterranean for duties in and around the Sea of Marmora.
	August. Passed through Dardanelles, torpedoing an armed steamer off the Gulf of Artaki. Later in the month she destroyed a further steamer off Mudania pier.
	November. Entered Straits of Marmora, incidents during this month included the bombardment of Mudania with her 6 pdr gun.
	December. Ordered to remain on patrol at the entrance to the Dardanelles. At the time the battle cruiser *Goeben* and light cruiser *Breslau* were moored in Constantinople Harbour, providing a continual threat to Mediterranean shipping. This was to be the primary role of the E.2 until January 1918. At that point she was forced to desert the Dardanelles as the result of a broken shaft.
1919	Withdrawn from active service in the Mediterranean and paid off at Malta dockyard.
1921	7 March. Sold to the Maltese ship breaking firm of Zammit.

LOWESTOFT   'Birmingham' class second class cruiser.

5,440 tons; 430′ x 50′ x 16′; 25½ knots; complement 400
Armament 9 x 6″ QF, 1 x 3″ AA, 2 x 21″ TT.

Laid down July, 1912; launched 23 April, 1913.

1914	21 April. Commissioned at Chatham for 1st Light Cruiser Squadron, Home/Grand Fleet.
	28 August. Involved in Battle of Heligoland Bight.
1915-16	2nd Light Cruiser Squadron, Grand Fleet.
1916	Transferred to Mediterranean.
1917	Refitted at Malta. Completed January 1918.
1918-19	8th Light Cruiser Squadron. Adriatic.
1919	16 September. Recommissioned for 6th Light Cruiser Squadron and placed on Africa station until 1929.
1930	January. Paid off at Devonport.

ATTENDANT   RFA Oiler.

1,935 tons; 200' x 34' x 15'; 8 knots.

Laid down 7 October, 1912; launched 5 July, 1913.

1914-19	Dockyard fuelling service.
1920	Held at Chatham in Reserve.
1921	January. Sheerness. In commission.
1922-23	Dockyard service, Rosyth.
1926	Held in Reserve at Rosyth.
1935	Sold to R.W. McLellan Ltd for £2,722 and later re-sold to Hemsley, Bell and Co. for further trading.
1939-45	On charter to Admiralty.
1941	1 January. Struck a mine whilst off Sheerness, but not seriously damaged.
1945	Returned to owner, being used in the South-East area as a bunkering ship.
1948	Transferred to British-Mexican petroleum.
1956	Broken up.

E.7   E-class submarine.

662 tons; 181' x 22½' x 12'; 16/10 knots; complement 30;
Armament 1 x 4"; 5 x 18" TT.

Laid down 1912; launched 2 October, 1913.

1914	Commissioned at Chatham for 8th (Portsmouth) Flotilla being transferred to Harwich on the outbreak of war.
	August. Numerous wide ranging patrols designed to prevent enemy warships approaching the B.E.F. convoys.
	December. Positioned to defend the sea plane carriers involved in the Cuxhaven air raid.
1915	June. After transfer to the Mediterranean, E.7 entered the Sea of Marmora.
	July. Wreaked considerable havoc upon Turkish shipping, even entering the harbour at Mudania and destroying the ammunition ship *Biga.* On other occasions, and whilst surfaced, an ammunition train and a troop train were both shelled.
	4 September. Left Mudros for a second patrol in the Sea of Marmora.
	5 September. Whilst passing through the Dardanelles, E.7 became ensnared in submarine netting and was later destroyed by a mine laid by Korvetten Kapitan von Heimburg of the German submarine UB-15. The crew of the E.7 managed to escape and were all imprisoned.

ARETHUSA   Name ship of class of light cruisers.

3,512 tons; 410' x 39' x 13½'; 27 knots; complement 270;
Armament 2 x 6" QF, 6 x 4" QF, 1 x 4" AA, 4 x 21" TT.

Laid down October, 1912; launched 25 October, 1913.
Amongst the nation's first light cruisers, being completely oil fired and having a particularly high speed. She was able to run down German destroyers in ordinary North Sea weather.

1914   11 August. Commissioned at Chatham for the Harwich destroyer force, acting as flotilla leader.

28 August. Battle of Heligoland Bight. In this, the *Arethusa* (flying Commodore Tyrwhitt's pennant) led the 3rd Flotilla of sixteen destroyers in a sweep through the Heligoland Bight, causing much damage to vessels operating in the area. During this operation the *Arethusa* was fired upon by the enemy cruisers *Stettin* and *Frauenlob,* later engaging the *Frauenlob* in a more sustained engagement. Although inflicting much damage on the German cruiser, the *Arethusa,* herself, had to be towed home. Eleven of her crew were killed and sixteen wounded.

1915   24 January. Participated in the Battle of Dogger Bank.

Later in the year *Arethusa* was transferred to the 5th Light Cruiser Squadron which was also operating out of Harwich.

1916   11 February. Whilst near Harwich struck a mine previously laid by UC-7. Subsequently drifting onto a nearby shore, she broke her back.

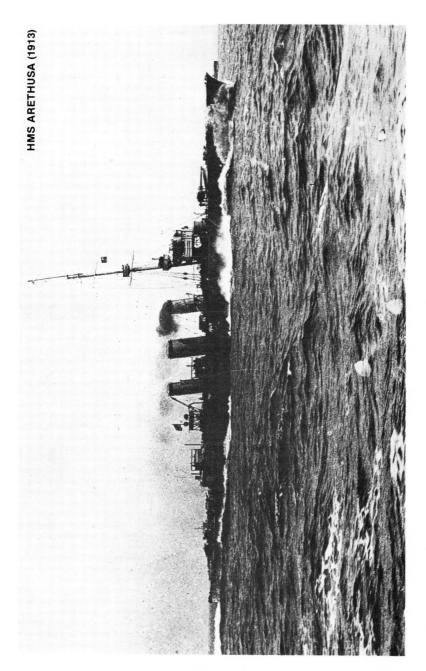

HMS ARETHUSA (1913)

E.8   E-class submarine.

662 tons; 181' x 22½' x 12'; 16/10 knots; complement 30;
Armament 1 x 4", 5 x 18" TT.

Laid down 1913; launched 30 October, 1913.

1914	Attached to 8th (Harwich) Flotilla.
	August. Conducting special patrols to protect the BEF convoys crossing to France. Later took up position prior to the Battle of Heligoland Bight.
1915	January. Covering the Elbe River area following the surface action off Dogger Bank.
	August. Detached to the Baltic. Under the command of Lt-Cdr Goodhart she had a difficult passage through the Copenhagen/ Malmo Straits, damaging a propeller whilst edging along the bottom in shallow waters. In all, the journey from Harwich to the Baltic took a week.
	October. Early in the month she captured the steamer *Margarette* and, on the 23rd, destroyed the 9,000 ton cruiser *Prinz Adalbert,* flagship of the German Baltic squadron.
1916	Operating out of the Port of Reval, on the Gulf of Finland, throughout the summer period.
1917	Operational base moved from Reval to Helsinki in order to avoid the effects of the revolution then taking place in Russia. Even so, operations had to cease towards the end of the year.
1918	8 April. Under treaty of Brest-Litovsk all British submarines in the Baltic had to be handed over to the Germans. Rather than accept this, the E.8 was scuttled just off Helsinki. (See E.1.)

SERVITOR   RFA Oiler.

1,935 tons; 200' x 34' x 15'; 8 knots.

Laid down 21 July, 1913; launched 26 May, 1914.
A similar class of vessel to the *Attendant.*

1915	May. Placed on dockyard service, mostly Firth of Forth.
1920	April. At Rosyth for paying off.
1921	January. Paid off at Sheerness.
1922	Sold out of Fleet service for £5,000.
1924	Owned by J. Le Masurier of London, having been re-named *Puloe Brani.*
1968	Having passed through a great number of hands she was, by this year, owned by Michigan Tankers Incorporated, having been re-named *Detroit.*

E.12   E-class submarine.

662 tons; 181 ' x 22½ ' x 12'; 16/10 knots; complement 30;
Armament 1 x 4", 5 x 18" TT.

Laid down 1913; launched 5 September, 1914.

1914	Commissioned for 8th (Harwich) Flotilla.
1915	May. Detached to Mediterranean.
	June. Carried out first patrol in Sea of Mamora during which time the E.12 destroyed or seriously damaged three Turkish steamers. This particular patrol was cut short due to engine trouble.
	September-October. Carried out a second patrol in the Sea of Marmora. Claimed four steamers and thirty sailing vessels.
1916-18	Patrols mainly restricted to Mediterranean, and aimed at countering the increasing U-boat menace.
1919	Malta dockyard and paid off.
1921	March. Sold to the Maltese ship breaking firm of Zammit.

E.13   E-class submarine.

662 tons; 181 ' x 22½ ' x 12'; 16/10 knots; complement 30.
Armament 1 x 4", 5 x 18" TT.

Laid down 1913; launched 22 September, 1914.

1914	Commissioned for 8th (Harwich) Flotilla.
1915	Detached to Baltic.
	14 August. Left Harwich for Baltic.
	18 August. Due to compass failure ran aground on the Saltholm sand bank, and within Danish territorial waters. Subsequently destroyed after being fired upon by two German destroyers. Reports also indicate that the crew were additionally machine gunned as they swam ashore.
1921	December. The wreck of the E.13 sold to Peterson and Albeck, a Danish scrap metal firm.

CALLIOPE   Name ship of class of light cruisers.

3,750 tons; 420' x 41½' x 14'; 29 knots; complement 301;
Armament 2 x 6" QF, 8 x 4" QF (later 4 x 6" QF, 2 x 3" AA).

Laid down January, 1914; launched 17 December, 1914.

1915	Commissioned at Chatham for the 4th Light Cruiser Squadron of the Grand Fleet.
1916	May. Present at Battle of Jutland (flying pennant of Commodore Le Mesurier). Towards the end of the day came under fire from the battleships of the German Third Squadron. Severely damaged.
1918	Rearmed.
1920	25 March. Commissioned at Devonport for 8th Light Cruiser Squadron on American and West Indies station.
1921	January. Paid off at Chatham.
	10 October. Commissioned at Chatham for Nore Reserve.
1926	25 April. Paid off at Chatham for refit.
1927	16 December. Commissioned at Chatham. Flagship, Nore Reserve.
1928	3rd Cruiser Squadron, Mediterranean.
1929	Paid off and entered Portsmouth Reserve.
1931	August. Sold to Ward of Inverkeithing.

CONQUEST   'Caroline' class light cruiser.

3,750 tons; 420' x 41½' x 14'; 29 knots; complement 301;
Armament 2 x 6" QF, 8 x 4" QF, 8 x 21" TT.

Laid down March, 1914; launched 20 January, 1915.

1915	Commissioned at Chatham for the 5th Light Cruiser Squadron operating out of Harwich.
1916	24 April. Fired upon by battle cruisers of the Grand Fleet during an attack upon the East Coast. Damaged following a direct hit from a 12-inch shell. Twenty-five crew members killed and a further thirteen wounded.
1917-18	Remained with the 5th Light Cruiser Squadron until the end of the war.
1919	Entered Nore Reserve.
1922	17 February. Commissioned for senior officer of 1st Submarine Flotilla, Atlantic Fleet.
1926	With 1st Submarine Flotilla in Mediterranean.
1928	7 April. Entered Portsmouth Reserve.
1930	29 August. Sold to 'Metal Industries' of Rosyth.

F.1   F-class submarine.

353 tons; 147½' x 16' x 15'; 14/9 knots; complement 18;
Armament 1 x 2 pdr, 3 x 18" TT.

Laid down 1 December, 1913; launched 31 March, 1915.
Only one of this class was built at Chatham, the order being placed prior to the
outbreak of war. Had a surface range of 3,000 miles.

1915	Commissioned at Chatham for 8th (Harwich) Flotilla.
1915-16	Transferred to 4th (Dover) Flotilla.
1916-17	Serving with the 8th (Yarmouth) Flotilla.
1917-18	Again transferred, this time to the 1st (Portsmouth) Flotilla.
1918-19	Placed on training duties. Campbeltown.
1920	Portsmouth dockyard. Broken up.

HMS G1 (1915)

G.1 G-class submarine.

700 tons; 185′ x 22½′ x 18′; 14½/10 knots; complement 31;
Armament 1 x 3″, 4 x 18″ TT, 1 x 21″ TT.

Laid down 1 October, 1914; launched 14 August, 1915.
First submarine in the Royal Navy to carry 21-inch torpedoes, the G.1 had a
surface range of 2,400 miles.

1915   Commissioned at Chatham for 2nd (Portsmouth) Flotilla.
1916   Transferred to 11th (Blyth) Flotilla.
1920   14 February. Sold to the Sunderland shipbreaking firm of B. Fryer.

G.4 G-class submarine.

700 tons; 185' x 22½' x 18'; 14½/10 knots; complement 31;
Armament 1 x 3", 4 x 18" TT, 1 x 21" TT.

Laid down 12 October, 1914; launched 23 October, 1915.

1916	Commissioned for 11th (Blyth) Flotilla.
	19 June. Sunk the German steamer *Ems* by gunfire.
1917-18	Patrolling North Sea. Frequently engaged in combatting the German U-boat menace.
1919	Serving with 5th (Atlantic) Flotilla.
1919-26	Portsmouth Reserve.
1928	June. Sold to Cashmore of Newport for breaking up.

G.5 G-class submarine.

700 tons; 185' x 22½' x 18'; 14½/10 knots; complement 31;
Armament 1 x 3", 4 x 18" TT, 1 x 21" TT.

Laid down 12 October, 1914; launched 23 November, 1915.

1916	Commissioned at Chatham for 11th (Blyth) Flotilla. Engaged throughout duration of war on North Sea patrols, frequently in an anti-submarine capacity.
1919	Short period with the 5th (Atlantic) Flotilla before entering Portsmouth Reserve.
1922	October. Sold to Cashmore of Newport for breaking up.

G.2 G-class submarine.

700 tons; 185' x 22½' x 18'; 14½/10 knots; complement 31;
Armament 1 x 3", 4 x 18" TT, 1 x 21" TT.

Laid down 1 October, 1914; launched 23 December, 1915.

1916	Commissioned for 11th (Blyth) Flotilla. Engaged throughout duration of war on North Sea patrols, frequently in an anti-submarine capacity. Most notable success occurred in May 1918 when the G.2 successfully torpedoed the U-78.
1919	Paid off and placed on sale list.
1920	January. Sold to B. Fryer of Sunderland.

G.3 G-class submarine.

700 tons; 185' x 22½' x 18'; 14½/10 knots; complement 31;
Armament 1 x 3", 4 x 18" TT, 1 x 21" TT.

Laid down 1 October, 1914; launched 22 January, 1916.

1916	Commissioned at Chatham for 11th (Blyth) Flotilla. Engaged for duration of war on North Sea patrols, mainly anti-submarine duties.
1919	Short period with 5th (Atlantic) Flotilla before entering Portsmouth Reserve.
1921	November. Sold to Young of Sunderland.

HAWKINS   Name ship of class of light cruisers.

9,750 tons; 565' x 65' x 17½'; 31 knots; complement 712
Armament 7 x 7.5", 4 x 3" AA, 6 x 12 pdr; 6 x 21" TT.

Laid down June, 1916; launched 1 October, 1917.
Ordered in December 1915, she was completed too late to see any service
during World War One.

1919	24 July. Commissioned at Chatham as Flagship to the 5th Cruiser Squadron on the China station.
1928	Returned to Chatham for a refit.
1929	Commissioned for the 2nd Cruiser Squadron, then in the Atlantic.
1931	May. Portsmouth. Entered Reserve prior to a refit.
1932	21 September. Commissioned at Portsmouth as Flagship to the 4th Cruiser Squadron on the East Indies station.
1938	Paid off at Portsmouth and entered Reserve.
1939	September-December. Rearming at Portsmouth.
1940-41	Flagship, South Atlantic.
1941	March. Transferred to East Indies.
1942	April. Completed refit at Portsmouth and joined 5th Cruiser Squadron.
1943	July-August. Refit at Simonstown.
1944	March. Nominally attached to 1st Cruiser Squadron of the Home Fleet whilst undergoing repairs on the Clyde. Later transferred to Rosyth command for conversion to training ship. The conversion, however, was never completed.
1945	June. Reduced to Reserve.
	September. Laid up at Falmouth.
1947	Re-located to Portsmouth for target trials.
	August. Broken up at Dalmuir.

R.1   R-class submarine.

410 tons; 163' x 16' x 11½ '; 9½/15 knots; complement 22;
Armament 6 x 18" TT.

Laid down 4 December, 1917; launched 25 April, 1918.
Designed for anti-submarine operations, the four R-class submarines built at
Chatham were completed too late to have any real impact on the war.

1918	Commissioned at Chatham for 14th (Blyth) Flotilla.
1919	Transferred to 4th Flotilla operating with the Atlantic Fleet.
1920	Paid off and entered Portsmouth Reserve.
1923	Sold for breaking up.

R.2   R-class submarine.

410 tons; 163' x 16' x 11½ '; 9½/15 knots; complement 22;
Armament 6 x 18" TT.

Laid down 4 December, 1917; launched 25 April, 1918.

1918	Commissioned at Chatham for 14th (Blyth) Flotilla.
1919	Transferred to Portsmouth Submarine School.
1923	February. Sold for breaking up.

R.3   R-class submarine.

410 tons; 163' x 16' x 11½'; 9½/15 knots; complement 22;
Armament 6 x 18" TT.

Laid down 4 December, 1917; launched 8 June, 1918.
1919   Portsmouth Torpedo School.
1919-23   Portsmouth Reserve.
1923   February. Sold for breaking up.

R.4   R-class submarine.

410 tons; 163' x 16' x 11½; 9½/15 knots; complement 22;
Armament 6 x 18" TT.

Laid down 4 December, 1917; launched 8 June, 1918.
1919-20   Portsmouth Submarine School.
1920-24   Portland Periscope School.
1924-32   6th (Portland) Flotilla.
1932-34   5th (Portsmouth) Reserve.
1934   May. Sold for breaking up.

HMS R3 (1918)

X.1   Submarine.

3,050 tons; 350′ x 29¾′ x 15¾′; 19½/9 knots; complement 110;
Armament 4 x 5.2″ QF, 6 x 21″ TT.

Laid down 2 November, 1921; launched 16 June, 1923.
Largest submarine ever built at Chatham, she was designed as a submarine
cruiser. Her 5.2-inch guns gave her the ability to surface and engage enemy
destroyers. The plan, though, was without success, the X.1 being far too slow
for such tactics to be successfully employed.

1925	Commissioned at Chatham for 5th (Portsmouth) Flotilla.
1926	Transferred to 1st (Mediterranean) Flotilla.
1930	Refitting at Chatham dockyard.
1931	Laid up in Portsmouth Reserve after repeated problems with the main engines.
1937	Broken up by Ward of Pembroke.

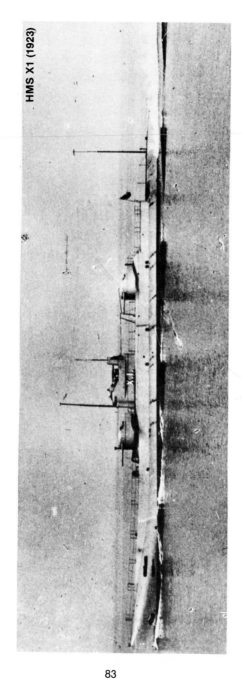

HMS X1 (1923)

KENT   Name ship of class of cruisers.

9,850 tons; 590′ x 68¼′ x 16¼′; 31½ knots; complement 784;
Armament 8 x 8″, 4 x 4″ QF HA, 4 x 3 pdr, 8 x 21″ TT.

Laid down 15 November, 1924; launched 16 March, 1926.
Largest cruiser to be constructed at Chatham.

1928	Commissioned at Chatham as Flagship of 5th Cruiser Squadron operating on the China station.
1930-31	Aircraft catapult fitted close to funnels. Capable of taking a Walrus, folding wing, aeroplane.
1932-33	Two single 4-inch HA guns added forward of funnels.
1937	Returned to Chatham for re-construction. Armour belt extended, internal armouring around machinery improved and some rearming undertaken.
1938	24 May. Recommissioned at Chatham and returned to previous duties on China station.
1939	December. Transferred to 4th Cruiser Squadron based on East Indies station.
1940	February-March. Refit, Colombo dockyard.
	August. Operating with 4th Cruiser Squadron in the Mediterranean. Convoy protection duties.
	18 September. Whilst east of Bardiyah, North Africa, she was extensively damaged after an attack mounted by two torpedo aircraft. Struck under the 'Y' turret, jamming the rudder. Emergency repairs undertaken at Alexandria before transfer to the dockyard at Simonstown.
	November. Left Simonstown bound for the dockyard at Devonport. Throughout most of the following year she was to remain in dockyard hands.
1941	21 April. Durng an air raid on the city of Plymouth, *Kent* was struck by a bomb that exploded astern of 'Y' turret.
	29 April. Suffered splinter damage during a further air raid upon Plymouth.
	September. Left Devonport to join 1st Cruiser Squadron of the Home Fleet. Employed in northern waters, protecting Russian convoys.
1942	August-November. Refit at Liverpool.
1944	5 December. Collided with *Blue Ranger.* Damage to *Kent* consisted of a 4′ x 1½′ hole torn into the starboard side just above the upper deck. Repairs undertaken on Clyde. Following their completion she was retained at Gareloch as flagship of the Reserve Fleet.
1946	October. Flagship of Chatham Reserve.
1947	June-July. Still at Chatham. Armament removed and transferred to Category 'C' Reserve. Later used for target trials.
1948	January. Sold for breaking up and removed to Troon.

HMS KENT (1926)

OBERON   **'O' class Patrol Submarine.**

1,311 tons; 269½' x 28' x 15½'; 13¾/7½ knots; complement 54;
Armament 1 x 4" QF, 8 x 21" TT.

Laid down March, 1924; launched 24 September, 1926.
A prototype overseas patrol submarine, she was the first true post-war design.

1926	Commissioned at Chatham for 5th (Portsmouth) Flotilla.
1931	Transferred to 1st (Mediterranean) Flotilla.
1934	Returned to 5th (Portsmouth) Flotilla.
1937	Reduced to Portsmouth Reserve.
1939	1 September. Recommissioned for 5th (Portsmouth) Flotilla but transferred later in the month to the 2nd (Dundee) Flotilla.
1940	7th (Clyde) Flotilla; 7th (Rothesay) Flotilla.
1942	March. Returned to Portsmouth for refit.
1943	February. Training duties with 7th (Rothesay) Flotilla.
1944	March. Training duties with 6th (Blyth) Flotilla.
	June. Paid off.
1945	August. Sold for breaking up.

ODIN   **'O' class Patrol Submarine.**

1,475 tons; 269½' x 30' x 16'; 17½/8 knots; complement 53;
Armament 1 x 4" QF, 8 x 21" TT.

Laid down 1927; launched 5 May, 1928.
An improved *Oberon,* with a much higher speed.

1929	Commissioned at Chatham for 3rd (Portsmouth) Flotilla.
1931	Transferred to 4th (China) Flotilla.
1939	October. Operating out of Colombo with the 8th Flotilla.
1940	May. With the threat of an Italian declaration of war the *Odin,* together with other submarines of the 8th Flotilla were dispatched to the Mediterranean and joined with the 4th (Singapore) Flotilla to form the new 1st Flotilla. The *Odin,* based on Malta, made her first patrol in June.
	13 June. Sunk by the Italian destroyer *Strale* whilst in the Gulf of Taranto.

HMS ODIN (1928)

PARTHIAN   'P' class patrol submarine.

1,740 tons; 260' x 29' x 16; 17½/8 knots; complement 56;
Armament 1 x 4" QF, 8 x 21" TT.

Laid down 1928; launched 22 June, 1929.
Similar to *Odin,* but with higher speed and a few other minor improvements.

1930   Commissioned for the 5th (Portsmouth) Flotilla.

1931   Attached to 4th (China) Flotilla.

1940   May. Transferred to Alexandria, operating with the newly formed 1st Flotilla whose main concern was that of cutting Italian communications with Tripoli.

    19 June. Entering Tobruk harbour she unsuccessfully attacked the old Italian cruiser *San Giorgio.*

    20 June. Made first successful British submarine attack in Mediterranean when she destroyed the Italian submarine *Diamante* whilst thirty miles north of Tobruk.

    16 July. Undertook first submarine landing operation in Mediterranean when a British agent was dispatched in Gromino Bay, Crete.

    31 August. Unsuccessfully attacked two 'Zara' class cruisers.

1941   9 January. Whilst patrolling off Cape Spartivento she torpedoed and sank the 4,208 ton *Carlo Martinolich.*

    25 June. Attacked and sank Vichy submarine *Souffleur.*

    August. Sent to the USA for a refit. Completed March 1942.

1942   April. Returned to the 1st (Mediterranean) Flotilla but later in the year transferred to the 8th (Gibraltar) Flotilla. Patrols continued to be aimed at cutting Italian communications. One exploit at this time included the shelling of a resin factory on the Aegean coastline of Greece.

    November. During operation Torch her designated role was that of preventing Italian warships interfering with the Allied landings.

1943   May. Operations in North Aegean, sunk several caiques and bombarded the railway near Platamore. Damaged a signal box and several railway wagons.

    August. Lost whilst in the Southern Adriatic. Cause uncertain, but probably hit a mine either in her patrol area or on passage to Beirut where she had been based since March.

RAINBOW   R-class Patrol Submarine.

1,740 tons; 260' x 30' x 16'; 17½/9 knots; complement 51;
Armament 1 x 4" QF, 8 x 21" TT.

Laid down 1929; launched 14 May, 1930.
Designed specifically for service in the Far East.

1932	Commissioned at Chatham for the 4th (China) Flotilla.
1940	July. With the worsening situation in Europe, combined with a high loss of submarines, she was attached to the 1st Flotilla in the Mediterranean.
	19 October. Whilst carrying out a patrol off the Southern coast of Italy, *Rainbow* was destroyed by the Italian submarine *Toti*.

SHOREHAM   Name ship of class of sloops.

1,105 tons; 250' x 35' x 10½'; 16½ knots; complement 100;
Armament 1 x 4" QF (later HA), 4 x 3 pdr (later replaced by 1 x 2 pdr and 3 x 20mm).

Laid down 1929; launched 22 November, 1930.
A replacement to the earlier 'Flower' class sloops of World War One, the 'Shoreham' class was specifically designed for foreign service and mine sweeping.

1931	27 October. Commissioned at Chatham for Persian Gulf.
1938	Detached temporarily to Mediterranean during Munich crisis.
1939-42	Remained in Middle East throughout early part of war. Involved in general escort duties.
1942	March. Transferred to Ceylon Escort Force.
1943	March. Returned to Mediterranean on a temporary basis, providing additional protection during the Sicily landings.
1944	March-June. Refitted at Cape Town.
	November. Returned to East Indies Escort Force.
1945	January. Present at capture of Akyab on the West coast of Burma.
	May-July. Refitted at Simonstown.
	September. Ordered to Persian Gulf.
1946	September. Paid off at Devonport and placed on sale list.
	October. Sold into mercantile service and re-named *Jorge Fel Joven*.

ROCHESTER   'Shoreham' class sloop.

1,105 tons; 250' x 35' x 10½'; 16½ knots; complement 100;
Armament 2 x 4" QF (later HA), 4 x 3 pdr (later replaced by 20mm).

Laid down 1930; undocked 16 July, 1931.

1932	24 March. Commissioned at Chatham for Africa station.
1939	Shortly before the declaration of war she was transferred to the East Indies, then sent to Liverpol in December.
1940	For virtually the rest of the war *Rochester* was employed on convoy escort duties attached, initially, to the Liverpool command, before transfer to the Derry command (in November 1941.) Amongst other units, she served with the 2nd Escort Division (Liverpool), the North-Eastern Escort Group (Liverpool) and the 37th and 39th Escort Groups (Derry).
	March-April. Repairs undertaken at Barrow following a collision with the steamship *Longford*. Accident occurred on 27th March when the *Rochester* received underwater damage.
	June-August. Refit at Liverpool.
1941	November. Operating out of Derry.
1942	6 February. Whilst off the Azores shared the sinking of U-82 with the *Tamarisk*.
1943	April-June. Refit on the Humber.
	July. Whilst off the Canaries shared the sinking of U-135 with the *Mignonette*.
1944	31 May. Whilst in heavy fog collided with the *Hart*. Received minor damage, and subsequently taken into Devonport dockyard for repair.
	August. Transferred to Plymouth command, serving with the 41st Escort Group.
	November. Start of three month refit undertaken on the Tyne.
1945	April. Transferred to Portsmouth Navigation School. This marked an end to active service, remaining attached to the school until 1950.
1951	6 January. Sold to Clayton and Davie for breaking up.

CHALLENGER   Survey ship.

1,140 tons; 220' x 36' x 12½'; 12½ knots; complement 84;

Laid down 1930; undocked 1 June, 1931.

1932	15 March. Completed at Portsmouth.
1933-39	Survey duties. Employed mostly around UK coast, but also the West and East Indies.
1939	Upon the outbreak of war she was placed under the command of the Home Fleet. Based initially at Portsmouth she was transferred to Nore Command in 1942.
1942-45	During these years *Challenger* saw service with the Eastern Fleet, being attached to the East Indies and, later, the Australia station.
1946	January. At Hong Kong, being prepared for a return trip to the UK. May-June. Retained at Chatham.
1947	Surveying Persian Gulf.
1949	Refit at Chatham.
1950	Surveying West Indies and Far East.
1953	Returned to UK and retained at Portsmouth.
1954	January. Broken up at Dover.

HMS CHALLENGER (1932

SWORDFISH   Name ship of class of Patrol Submarine.

735 tons; 193' x 24' x 12'; 13¾/10 knots; complement 38;
Armament 1 x 3" HA, 6 x 21" TT.

Laid down December 1930; launched 10 November, 1931.
A saddle tank type submarine intended for training and patrols in confined
waters.

1932	Commissioned at Chatham for 5th (Portsmouth) Flotilla.
1935	Transferred to Home Fleet, operating with the 3rd and then the 2nd Submarine Flotilla.
1939	On the outbreak of war *Swordfish* was based at Portland but transferred the following month to Dundee. Throughout the rest of her service career she was based at various East Coast bases (Rosyth, Blyth and Harwich) undertaking a series of patrols in the North Sea, English Channel and Biscay.
1940	16 November. Sunk in Bay of Biscay. Cause unknown.

STURGEON   'Swordfish' class Patrol Submarine.

735 tons; 193' x 24' x 12'; 13¾/10 knots; complement 38;
Armament 1 x 3" HA, 6 x 21" TT.

Laid down 3 January, 1931; launched 8 January, 1932.

1932-39	Attached to various submarine flotillas, being based at Portsmouth (1932), Portland (1933-35) and Dundee (1939).
1939	Shortly after the outbreak of war the *Sturgeon* was transferred to the 2nd (Rosyth) Flotilla for North Sea operations.
	14 September. Fired. in error, three torpedoes at *Swordfish*, fortunately without result.
1940	Attached to the 6th (Blyth) Flotilla.
1941	20 March. Torpedoed the 3,000 ton tanker *Drafn* whilst patrolling off Stanlandet.
1942	Operating out of the Clyde.
	March. Operated as beacon during St. Nazaire raid.
1943	April. Attached to the 7th (Rothesay) Flotilla.
	May-August. Devonport. Refit.
	11 October. Lent to Dutch navy and re-named *Zeehond.* Used mainly for the training of Dutch crews in anti-submarine warfare.
1944	April-October. Based at Rothesay.
1945	September. Returned to Royal Navy.
1946	Sold out of naval service and eventually arrived at Granton for breaking up.

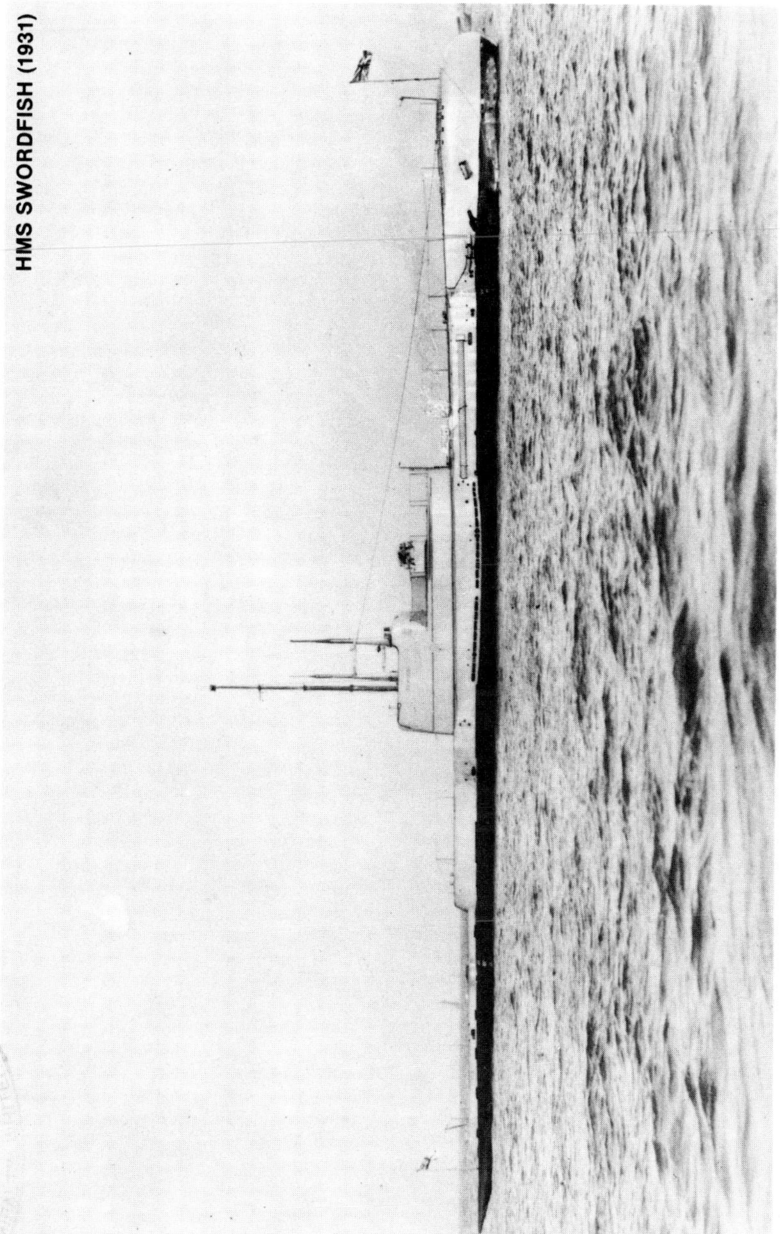

HMS SWORDFISH (1931)

GUARDIAN   Netlayer.

2,860 tons; 310′ x 53′ x 13′; 18 knots; complement 181;
Armament 2 x 4″ HA.

Laid down 15 October, 1931; launched 1 September, 1932.
Designed for netlaying and fleet photography.

1933	13 June. Commissioned at Chatham for Home Fleet.
1936	Detached to Mediterranean during period of Abyssinia crisis.
1941	August. Rosyth command before joining East Indies station in October. For the next three and a half years the *Guardian* was the Mediterranean alternately at Malta and Oran.
1945	January. Attached to the British Pacific Force.
1946	December. Held at Trincomalee preparatory to her return to the UK.
1947-61	Held in Reserve.
1962	December. Arrived at Troon for breaking up.

DUNDEE   'Shoreham' class sloop.

1,105 tons; 250′ x 35′ x 10½′; 16½ knots; complement 100;
Armament 2 x 4″ QF.

Laid down 1931; undocked 20 September, 1932.

1933	23 March. Commissioned at Chatham for America and West Indies station. Remained under this command throughout her service career.
1940	15 September. Sunk by U-48.

SEAHORSE   'Swordfish' class Patrol Submarine.

640 tons; 193′ x 24′ x 12′; 13¾/10 knots; complement 38;
Armament 1 x 3″, 6 x 21″ TT.

Laid down 14 September, 1931; launched 15 November, 1932.

1933	Commissioned for 5th (Portsmouth) Flotilla, being transferred to the 6th (Portland) Flotilla during the following year.
1936	Attached to Home Fleet.
1939	On the outbreak of war the *Seahorse* was transferred to Dundee for North Sea patrol duties. Later based at Rosyth and then Blyth.
1940	7 January. Sunk by a German minesweeper whilst in the Heligoland Bight.

STARFISH   'Swordfish' class patrol submarine.

640 tons; 193' x 24' x 12'; 13¾/10 knots; complement 38;
Armament 1 x 3", 6 x 21" TT.

Laid down 26 September, 1931; launched 14 March, 1933.

1933	Commissioned for 5th (Portsmouth) Flotilla, being transferred to the 6th (Portland) Flotilla during the following year.
1936	Attached to Home Fleet.
1939	On the outbreak of war the *Starfish* was transferred to Dundee for North Sea patrol duties. Later based at Rosyth and then Blyth.
1940	9 January. Sunk by the German minesweeper M.7 whilst in the Heligoland Bight.

ARETHUSA   Name ship of class of cruisers.

5,220 tons; 480′ x 51′ x 16½′; 32 knots; complement 500;
Armament 6 x 6″, 4 x 4″ HA, 6 x 21″ TT (one aeroplane later removed).

Laid down 25 January, 1933; launched 6 March, 1934.

1935	21 May. Commissioned for Mediterranean as flagship of the 3rd Cruiser Squadron. She was to remain in the Mediterranean until February 1940 when she was transferred to the 2nd Cruiser Squadron of the Home Fleet.
1940	August-September. Refit at Chatham. Whilst in dry dock, and much to the consternation of the Chatham work force, she used her 4-inch anti-aircraft guns upon bombers approaching London.
	27 October. Having returned to the Home Fleet she was involved in a collision with an unknown merchantman, receiving damage to her stern.
	October-November. Repairs undertaken on Tyne.
	November. Detached to Nore command and moored close to Tower Bridge as part of London's anti-aircraft barrage.
1942	February. Transferred to 15th Cruiser Squadron, Mediterranean.
	18 November. Hit by an airborne torpedo whilst off the coast of North Africa. Received considerable damage. A and B turrets put out of action, serious fires destroyed most of her forward electrical circuits whilst many of her bulkheads were flooded to the upper deck level. Towed into Alexandria by two destroyers.
1943	Most of this year spent under repair. Alexandria could only undertake temporary repairs. was then taken across the Atlantic for more extensive repairs at Charleston. Out of action for 12½ months.
1944	January. Refit. Chatham.
	April. Rejoined Home Fleet. Part of 1st Cruiser Squadron.
	24 June. Whilst in northern waters she received minor damage as the result of an air attack.
	25 June. Further, more extensive damage, when a delayed action bomb exploded nearby. Y magazine flooded.
	July-November. Sent to Clyde for repairs.
1945	Attached to 15th Cruiser Squadron, Mediterranean, until end of war.
	27 October. Left Trieste, returning to Chatham in order to enter Nore Reserve.
1946	February. Plans considered for her transfer to the Royal Norwegian Navy. Later cancelled.
	May. Reduced to Category 'B' Reserve.
1950	Sold out of naval service and subseqently broken up.

HMS ARETHUSA (1934)

SHARK   Name ship of class of patrol submarines.

670 tons; 193' x 24' x 12'; 14/10 knots; complement 39;
Armament 1 x 3", 6 x 21" TT.

Laid down 12 June, 1933; launched 31 May, 1934.

1934	Commissioned at Chatham for 5th (Portsmouth) Flotilla but transferred to Mediterranean during the following year.
1939	October. Returned to 5th (Portsmouth) Flotilla and undertook patrol duties in Channel and Bay of Biscay.
	December. Transferred to 3rd (Harwich) Flotilla to strengthen Royal Navy efforts at denying German access to North Sea and Norwegian coastal areas.
1940	May. Based at Rosyth.
	6 July. Sunk by German minesweeper whilst off the coast of Norway. Having surfaced during day light she had been sighted and depth charged by German aircraft. Sustaining considerable damage she had been forced to remain on the surface fighting off further attacks until all her ammunition was expended. Later captured, her crew was imprisoned prior to her sinking.

SNAPPER   'Shark' class patrol submarine.

670 tons; 193' x 24' x 12'; 14/10 knots; complement 39;
Armament 1 x 3", 6 x 21" TT.

Laid down 18 September, 1933; launched 25 October, 1934.

1935	Commissioned for Home Fleet but transferred to Mediterranean the following year.
1939	As with *Shark,* transferred to 5th (Portsmouth) Flotilla shortly after outbreak of war. Operating from Harwich by the end of the year.
1940	January-February. Refit at Chatham.
	May. Based at Rosyth and patrolling Norwegian coastline.
	3 July. Sank the German merchant vessel *Cygnus.*
	November. Transferred to 6th (Blyth) Flotilla.
1941	12 February. Sunk in Bay of Biscay. Cause unknown.

HMS SNAPPER (1934)

DEPTFORD 'Grimsby' class sloop.

990 tons; 266′ x 36′ x 10′; 16½ knots; complement 100;
Armament 2 x 4.7″ QF, 1 x 3″ HA (later removed), 4 x 3 pdr (removed and later
replaced by 6 x 20mm).

Undocked 5 February, 1935.

1935	14 August. Commissioned at Portsmouth for East Indies.
1939	At the outbreak of war she was transferred to the Mediterranean, being brought back to Liverpool in December.
1940	January-July. Attached to 2nd Escort Division. Convoy protection duties in and around the Western Approaches.
	3 February. Collision with the 4,545 ton steamer *Antigone*, sustaining slight damage.
	March. Repairs undertaken at Liverpool.
	July-August. Attached to North-East Escort Force before transfer to the Liverpool Sloop Division (until August) but later seeing service with the 36th Escort Group.
	22 December. Extensive damage (torn plates and buckled frames) after a collision with *Stork*.
1942	January-August. Under repair at Liverpool.
1944	Operating in Mediterranean with 37th Escort Group based at Algiers.
	December. Returned to Portsmouth. Part of 38th Escort Group.
1945	De-commissioned at Milford and entered Reserve.
1948	Broken up by Ward of Milford Haven.

HMS GRAMPUS (1936)

GRAMPUS Name ship of class of mine laying submarines.

1,520 tons; 293′ x 25½′ x 17′; 15¾/8¾ knots; complement 59;
Armament 1 x 4″ QF, 6 x 21″ TT, 50 mines.

Laid down 20 August, 1934; launched 25 February, 1936.

1937	January. Undergoing trials at Chatham. Later in the year commissioned for 4th (China) Flotilla.
1940	May. Transferred to 1st (Mediterranean) Flotilla.
	24 June. Destroyed off the coast of Sicily by Italian torpedo boats *Circe* and *Clio*.

SUNFISH 'Shark' class patrol submarine.

670 tons; 193' x 24' x 12'; 14/10 knots; complement 39;
Armament 1 x 3", 6 x 21" TT.

Laid down 22 July, 1935; launched 30 September, 1936.

1937	Commissioned for 5th (Portsmouth) Flotilla.
1939	Shortly before the outbreak of war she was transferred to the North coast of Scotland, patrolling the Norwegian coastline. In December she joined the 3rd (Harwich) Flotilla.
1940	Throughout the year she was attached to various East coast bases (Harwich, Rosyth and Blyth).
1941	June-September. Refit. Tyne.
1942	January. Entered Portsmouth dockyard for extensive repairs.
1943	Upon completion of repairs in September she was placed on training duties at Rothesay.
1944	May. Lent to Soviet Navy as B.1 27 July. Mistakenly sunk by British aircraft during her passage to the Soviet Union. (A 90 mile navigation error was blamed).

STERLET 'Shark' class patrol submarine.

670 tons; 193' x 24' x 12'; 14/10 knots; complement 39;
Armament 1 x 3", 6 x 21" TT.

Laid down 1936; launched 22 September, 1937.

1938	Commissioned for 5th (Portsmouth) Flotilla.
1939	Transferred to North coast of Scotland just before the declaration of hostilities, joining the 3rd (Harwich) Flotilla in December.
1940	12 April. Unsuccessfully attacked convoy West of the Skaw. 15 April. Sank German gunnery ship *Brummer.* 16 April. Destroyed by German anti-submarine craft whilst continuing her patrol in the Skaggerack.

SEAL 'Shark' class patrol submarine.

670 tons; 193' x 24' x 12'; 14/10 knots; complement 39;
Armament 1 x 3", 6 x 21" TT.

Laid down 1937; launched 27 September, 1938.

1939	Commissioned for 5th (Portsmouth) Flotilla but transferred to Aden in September. Returned to Portsmouth in October.
1940	January. Transferred to 2nd (Rosyth) Flotilla. 2 May. Struck German mine whilst in Kattegat. Despite attempt to scuttle, she fell into German hands. Subsequently towed to Fredrikshavn.
1941	June. Condemned for scrap after German failure to recondition her.

EURYALUS   'Dido' class cruiser.

5,600 tons; 485' x 50½' x 16¾'; 32 knots; complement 480;
Armament 10 x 5.25", 8 x 2 pdr, 6 x 21" TT.

Laid down 21 October, 1937; launched 6 June, 1939.
Ordered under the 1936 Programme, *Euryalus* was the last cruiser built at
Chatham.

1941	June-July. Undergoing trials at Chatham.
	September. Whilst at Chatham 5 x 20mm guns added to her secondary armament. Commissioned for Mediterranean.
1943	October. Refit. Clyde.
1944	August. Attached to Home Fleet.
	4 September. Collided with *Black Ranger*. Damaged propeller blades.
	December. Flagship of 5th Cruiser Squadron and detached to East Indies.
1945	February. Joined British Pacific Fleet, arriving at Sydney on the 11th. Remained in the Far East for the next two years.
1947	February. Returned to UK and eventually de-commissioned at Rosyth.
1948	March. Commissioned for Mediterranean.
	16 April. Whilst berthing at Malta she was hit by a tug and sustained damage to starboard side.
1954	August. Entered Devonport Reserve.
1959	July. Arrived at Blyth for breaking up.

TIGRIS   T-class patrol submarine.

1,090 tons; 265' x 26½' x 14½'; 15¼/9 knots; complement 59;
Armament 1 x 4" QF, 10 x 21" TT.

Laid down 11 May, 1938; launched 31 October, 1939.
1940   May. Attached to 5th (Portsmouth) Flotilla for trials.
            July. Placed on North Sea patrols, operating with the 2nd (Rosyth)
            Flotilla.
            13 November. Sank the barque *Charles Edmond* whilst on patrol 60
            miles west of Gironde.
1941   February. Transferred to the Clyde and, from July, engaged upon
            patrols to support Russian operations in the Arctic.
1942   February-July. Refit at Devonport before returning to the Clyde and
            further Arctic patrols. In this second round of northern patrols
            unsuccessfully attacked *Koln* and *Scheer.*
            December. Transferred to 1st (Mediterranean) Flotilla based at
            Beirut.
1943   10 March. Disappeared in Gulf of Naples. Probably destroyed by an
            Italian mine.

TORBAY   T-class patrol submarine.

1,090 tons; 265' x 26½' x 14½'; 15¼/9 knots; complement 59;
Armament 1 x 4" QF, 10 x 21" TT (20mm Oerlikon added during war).

Laid down 21 November, 1938; launched 9 April, 1940.
Perhaps the most successful of all Chatham built submarines, having a
particularly varied war career.
1941   January. Sea trials undertaken with 2nd (Clyde) Flotilla, transferring
            to the 3rd (Clyde) Flotilla in February.
            April. Joined 1st (Mediterranean) Flotilla at Gibraltar. Her first
            patrol, undertaken during that month not particularly successful
            owing to a lack of drill. An attack upon a supply ship off Cape
            Ferrato failed when only one of three ordered torpedoes was
            actually fired.
            May. Operating out of Alexandria and conducting patrols in the
            Dardanelles and Aegean.
            6 June. Whilst off Cape Helles torpedoed the Vichy French tanker
            Alberta. As the vessel did not immediately sink she was later
            destroyed by gun fire.
            10 June. Successfully torpedoed the Italian tanker *Guiseppini
            Gherardi.*
            16 June. Returned to Alexandria having ended a particularly
            successful patrol that not only included the two tankers but,
            additionally, three caiques and the schooner *Gesu e Maria.*
            28 June-5 July. A further patrol in the Southern Aegean during

HMS TORBAY (continued)

which she sank two caiques, the merchantman *Citta di Tripoli* and the Italian submarine *Jantina*.

2-22 August. Her fourth Mediterranean patrol was chiefly characterised by a rescue of British troops stranded on Paxamadia Island, Crete.

1942   4 March. Whilst patrolling Ionian Sea she sighted a convoy of northbound troopships entering Corfu Roads. Entered the harbour and proceeded to make a daylight attack. The troopships, apparently only passing through, were no longer there, but two supply ships were damaged. During this action the *Torbay* was depth charged on numerous occasions. As a result Lt-Cdr A.C.C. Miers, commanding the *Torbay,* was awarded the V.C.

April. *Torbay's* last patrol under Lt-Cdr Miers. Chased a convoy on the 19th and destroyed a small tanker on the 21st. Returned to UK for a refit.

May-November. Temporarily assigned to 5th (Portsmouth) Flotilla, with refit undertaken at Devonport during the late summer and early autumn.

November. Work up patrols with 3rd (Clyde) Flotilla.

1943   January. Returned to Mediterranean carrying out her first, acclimatizing, patrol off Valencia. Now under the command of Lt R.J. Clutterbuck.

March. Operating out of Algiers she was ordered to patrol the Tyrrhenean Sea. Destroyed, during this month, the *Lillois* a merchantman of 3,681 tons.

18 April. Sustained internal damage during an air raid upon Algiers. Towed to Gibraltar for repairs.

August. Patrolling off Elba Operation 'Husky'.

16 October. During a patrol of the Aegean she destroyed the 1,925 ton German steamer *Kari.* Severely depth charged during this particular patrol.

November. Operating out of Beirut. A further successful patrol during which she sank a floating dock under tow and the German steamer *Palma* and a caique.

1944   March. Remained at Beirut throughout the winter period before returning to UK for a refit.

April-August. Refitting at Portsmouth.

August. Attached to 3rd (Holy Loch) Flotilla.

December. Nominally with 4th (East Indies) Flotilla.

1945   January. Joined 2nd (Trincomalee) Flotilla, operating with British Pacific Fleet.

7-21 April. Patrolling off coast of Sumatra during which time beach reconnaissance parties were landed.

June-July. Sank coaster and two junks in Malacca Strait.

October. Returned to UK.

December. Held at Portsmouth and eventually sold to Ward's of Britton Ferry for scrap.

UMPIRE   U-class patrol submarine.

540 tons; 191 ' x 16 ' x 15 '; 11/10 knots; complement 33;
Armament 1 x 12 pdr, 4 x 21 " TT.

Laid down 1 January, 1940; launched 30 December, 1940.
Part of war time emergency programme, the U-class submarines were built for
in-shore operations.

1941   May. Attached to 5th (Portsmouth) Flotilla for acceptance trials that
        were to be carried out in co-operation with the 3rd (Clyde) Flotilla.
        19 July. Whilst in the North Sea she was accidentally rammed and
        sunk by the armed trawler *Peter Hendriks*. At the time *Umpire* was
        on her way north to undertake sea trials with the 3rd (Clyde) Flotilla.

UNA   U-class patrol submarine.

540 tons; 191 ' x 16 ' x 15 '; 11/10 knots; complement 33;
Armament 1 x 12 pdr AA, 4 x 21 " TT.

Laid down 7 May, 1940; launched 10 June, 1941.

1941   September. Attached to the 5th (Portsmouth) Flotilla for sea trials.
        November. Transferred to Gibraltar. Operating with 8th Flotilla.
1942   January. Operating with 10th (Malta) Flotilla.
        13 March. Destroyed the 250 ton schooner *Maria Immacolata*.
        11/12 August. As an attempt at creating further security for
        Operation Pedestal, a group from the Special Boat Section was
        landed in Catania Bay for purposes of destroying airfield.
        Unfortunately the patrol was captured.
        November. At time of Operation Torch involved in patrols to prevent
        Italian ships interfering with the landings.
1943   1 February. Shelled two large schooners anchored off Hammamet.
        Action broken off when shore batteries opened fire.
        April. Returned to UK. During her time in the Mediterranean the *Una*
        had undertaken seventeen patrols.
        May-August. Refitting at Blyth.
        August. Placed on anti-submarine training duties until end of
        hostilities.
1945   November. Held in Reserve at Lisahally.
1949   April. Sold to E. Rees of Llanelly for breaking up.

SPLENDID   Improved S-class submarine.

715 tons; 202½ ' x 23¾ ' x 14'; 14¾/8 knots; complement 48;
Armament 1 x 3", 7 x 21" TT.

Laid down 7 March, 1941; launched 19 January, 1942.
Part of the war emergency programme, she was originally laid down as P.228
but given the name *Splendid* in March, 1943.

1942   August. Attached to 3rd (Clyde) Flotilla for trials.
          November. Transferred to Mediterranean, sinking the supply ship
          Luigi Favorita during her first patrol.
          18 December. Sank Italian destroyer *Aviere* after the original
          torpedo had missed a supply ship.
1943   January. During a particularly successful patrol she landed agents
          in Corsica going on to destroy the 765 ton *Commercio.*
          17 February. Whilst patrolling off Cape Vita she fired six torpedoes
          on a convoy of west bound ships, two hits. This patrol in connection
          with North African landings.
          11-28 March. During a patrol she torpedoed 3,177 ton tanker *Devoli*
          and the 4,887 ton tanker *Giorgio.*
          21 April. Damaged by German destroyer *Hermes.* Most of crew
          rescued when *Splendid* scuttled off coast of Corsica. In all, she had
          carried out six Mediterranean patrols, destroying 35,000 tons of
          shipping.

SPORTSMAN   Improved S-class patrol submarine.

715 tons; 202½' x 23¾' x 14'; 14¾/8 knots; complement 48;
Armament 1 x 3", 7 x 21" TT.

Laid down 1 July, 1941; launched 17 April, 1942.
Originally launched as submarine P.229 she was given the name *Sportsman* in March, 1943.

1942	March. Attached to 3rd (Clyde) Flotilla for both acceptance trials and active service.
1943	March. Transferred to Mediterranean being based at Algiers, Beirut and Malta.
1944	Returned to UK for refit, eventually being sent to Philadelphia for more extensive work to be completed.
1945	Attached to 3rd (Holy Loch) Flotilla before being placed on training duties on the conclusion of hostilities.
	December. Placed in Harwich Reserve.
1947	February-May. Refit at Chatham and then Reserve at Portsmouth.
1951	Lent to French Navy as *Sibylle*.
1952	23 September. Lost 38 miles East of Toulon, with all hands

HMS TRADEWIND (1942)

TRADEWIND   T-class (third group) patrol submarine.

1,090 tons; 265' x 26½' x 14½'; 15¼/9 knots; complement 61;
Armament 1 x 4" QF, 11 x 21" TT.

Laid down 11 February, 1942; launched 11 December, 1942.
A development of the earlier T-class with an operational depth of 350'. Capable of laying eighteen M2 mines.

1943	December. Attached to 3rd (Holy Loch) Flotilla for trials.
1944	March. Operating in Far East, initially based at Trincomalee but later part of British Pacific Fleet at Fremantle.
	19 September. Sank *Junyo Maru* with two torpedo.
1945	Returned to UK and taken in at Chatham for refit.
1946	June. Based at Portland.
1948	July. Returned to Chatham for modernisation. At this time she was specially fitted with a snort mast and underwent speed trials.
1954	Entered Portsmouth Reserve.
1955	December. Sold out of naval service for breaking up.

HMS SHALIMAR (1943)

SHALIMAR   Improved S-class patrol submarine.

715 tons; 202½ ' x 23¾ ' x 14'; 14¾/8 knots; complement 48;
Armament 1 x 3", 7 x 21" TT.

Laid down 1942; launched 22 April, 1943.

1944	March. Attached to 3rd (Holy Loch) Flotilla for trials.
	August. Operating out of Trincomalee.
1945	November. Returned to UK and entered Harwich Reserve.
1946	Lishally Reserve. Target trials ship until 1947.
1950	July. Purchased by West of Scotland Shipbreaking Co. broken up.

TRENCHANT   T-class (third group) patrol submarine.

1,090 tons; 265' x 26½ ' x 14½ '; 15¼/9 knots; complement 61;
Armament 1 x 4" QF, 11 x 21" TT.

Laid down 9 May, 1942; launched 24 March, 1943.

1944	Attached to 7th (Rothesay) Flotilla for trials.
	May. Transferred to Trincomalee operating with 4th Flotilla.
	5 August. Unsuccessfully attacked an escorted coaster.
	9 August. Intercepted same coaster and escorting mine layer. Took 14 prisoners after destroying vessels by gun fire.
	12 September. Landed special operations party in North Sumatra.
	27 October. Whilst carrying out a patrol in Malacca Straits she successfully attacked *Sumatra* and *Volpi.*
	21 December. A further patrol in Malacca Straits resulted in the destruction of two landing craft by gun fire.
1945	4 January. Bombarded Pulo Pandang.
	25 February. Attacked heavily defended convoy, sinking one coaster.
	4 March. In combined gun action with *Terrapin,* destroyed an enemy submarine chaser.
	8 June. Torpedoed and sunk the 12,700 ton Japanese cruiser, *Ashigara.*
	November. Returned to Portsmouth for refit.
1947	February. Entered Portsmouth Reserve.
1949-50	With 3rd (Rosyth) Flotilla.
1951-59	Based in Mediterranean.
1962	November. Chatham. Placed on sales list.
1963	July. Arrived at Faslane for breaking up.

MODESTE   Modified 'Black Swan' class sloop.

1,350 tons; 299½ ' x 38½ ' x 11 '; 19¾ knots; complement 192.
Armament 6 x 4″ QF, 4 x 40mm bofors (later reduced to 2).

Laid down 15 February, 1943; launched 29 January, 1944.
Specifically built for escort duties, both the *Modeste* and *Nereide* had a considerable anti-aircraft capability. Ordered under the 1941 Programme, their late completion date precluded a war time operational role. Re-classificed in 1947 as frigates.

1945	15 October. Entered Chatham Reserve after completion during the previous month.
1946	20 February. Commissioned at Chatham for gunnery training at Portsmouth. Later became tender to *Vernon,* the Portsmouth Torpedo School.
1950-52	Held in Reserve at Portsmouth.
1953	Far East service, having been commissioned for the 3rd Frigate squadron.
1956	Detached to Mediterranean as a result of the Suez crisis.
1958	Returned to Portsmouth Reserve.
1961	November. Arrived at St. David's for breaking up.

NEREIDE   Modified 'Black Swan' class sloop.

1,350 tons; 299½ ' x 38½ ' x 11 '; 19¾ knots; complement 192;
Armament 6 x 4″ QF, 4 x 40mm bofors.

Laid down 15 February, 1943; launched 29 January, 1944.
The last sloop to be built at Chatham.

1946	6 May. Completed. The end of hostilities removed any urgency that may have existed for an earlier completion date. Later that year she was commissioned for the South Atlantic.
1953	With the 7th Frigate Squadron in the West Indies.
1955	Placed in Reserve at Portsmouth.
1958	May. Arrived at Bo'Ness for breaking up.

TURPIN   T-class (third group) patrol submarine.

1,090 tons; 265' x 26½' x 14½'; 15¼/9 knots; complement 61.
Armament 1 x 4" QF, 11 x 21" TT.

Laid down 24 May, 1943; launched 5 August, 1944.

1944	December. Attached to 3rd (Holy Loch) Flotilla for trials.
	July. Operating with British Pacific Force out of Fremantle.
1947	January. Returned to Devonport for refit.
	May. Recommissioned for 5th (Portsmouth) Flotilla.
1950	December. Re-entered Chatham dockyard for a complete reconstruction programme.
1957	Commissioned for 2nd (Portland) Flotilla.
1958	March. Having developed engine trouble whilst operating in the Caribbean, she was towed to Devonport by the tug *Samsonia*. Arrived April 9.
1962	Attached to 5th (Mediterranean) Flotilla. Operating out of Malta she was one of the last submarines to use this island base.
1964	November. Returned to UK and entered Portsmouth Reserve.
1965	Transferred to Israeli Navy after an extensive refit and re-named *Leviathan*.

THERMOPYLAE   T-class (third group) patrol submarine.

1,090 tons; 265' x 26½' x 14½'; 15¼/9 knots; complement 61;
Armament 1 x 4" QF, 11 x 21" TT.

Laid down 26 October, 1943; launched 27 June, 1945.

1946	March. Joined 3rd (Holy Loch) Flotilla for trials.
1947-68	Remained in naval service receiving numerous refits at Chatham and Rosyth yards. Eventually placed on sale list in December 1968.
1970	July. Arrived at Troon, being broken up during the following year.

ACHERON   A-class patrol submarine.

1,120 tons; 221' x 22¼' x 17'; 18½/8 knots; complement 61.
Armament 1 x 4" QF (later removed), 10 x 21" TT.

Laid down 26 August, 1944; launched 25 March, 1947.
Designed for operations against the Japanese, having better living accommodation than previous boats.

1948-64	General naval service in UK. Detached to Middle East November-December 1959. Refits carried out 1950 and 1960 (Devonport) and 1952 and 1954 (Portsmouth).
1965-67	Lent to Royal Canadian Navy.
1972	August. Broken up at Newport by J. Cashmore Ltd.

VIDAL   Survey vessel.

1,940 tons; 297′ x 40′ x 10½′; 12 knots; complement 161;
Armament 4 x 3 pdr (saluting) and depth charges.
First surveying vessel to be equipped with a helicopter.

Laid down 5 July, 1950; launched 31 July, 1951.
1958-70   General surveying duties: West Indies (1958-1965) and Far East
(1966-1970). Refits during this period normally carried out at
Chatham.
1976   Sold out of naval service.

OBERON   Name ship of class of patrol submarine.

1,610 tons; 295′ x 26½′ x 18′; 12/17 knots; complement 68;
Armament 8 x 21″ TT.

Laid down 28 November, 1957; launched 18 July, 1959.
1961   24 February. Completed and attached to 3rd (Faslane) Flotilla. Still
in service 1982.

ONSLAUGHT   'Oberon' class patrol submarine.

1,610 tons; 295′ x 26½′ x 18′; 12/17 knots; complement 68;
Armament 8 x 21″ TT.

Laid down 8 April, 1959; launched 24 September, 1960.
Still in Service 1982.

OCELOT   'Oberon' class patrol submarine.

1,610 tons; 295′ x 26½′ x 18′; 12/17 knots; complement 68;
Armament 8 x 21″ TT.

Laid down 17 November, 1960; launched 5 May, 1962.
1964   Commissioned for 3rd (Faslane) Flotilla.
1967   Entered Rosyth dockyard for major refit.
1982   Still in service.

OJIBWA 'Oberon' class patrol submarine.

1,610 tons; 295' x 26½' x 18'; 12/17 knots; complement 68;
Armament 8 x 21" TT.

Laid down 27 September, 1962; launched 29 February, 1964.
1965   23 September. Commissioned at Halifax. First submarine to be
          refitted at HMC Dockyard in Halifax and to use the modern syncro-
          lift facilities.
1977   Deployed on Canada's west coast, Returned to east coast later in
          year.
1982   Completing mid-life refit, receiving new sonar, fire control,
          periscope, communications and navigation equipment.

ONONDAGA 'Oberon' class patrol submarine.

1,610 tons; 295' x 26½' x 18'; 12/17 knots; complement 68;
Armament 8 x 21" TT.

Laid down 18 June, 1964; launched 25 September, 1965.
1967   22 June. Commissioned at Halifax. Has since operated mainly from
          Halifax, making several trips to the UK and has carried out
          operations in the Caribbean.
1982   Undergoing mid-life refit at Halifax.

OKANAGAN 'Oberon' class patrol submarine.

1,610 tons; 295' x 26½' x 18'; 12/17 knots; complement 68;
Armament 8 x 21" TT.

Laid down 25 March, 1965; launched 17 September, 1966.
The last warship to be launched at Chatham. Since her launching the dockyard
has gone on to specialise in refit work. A special nuclear complex was
constructed for the 'Fleet' class submarines.
1968   22 June. Commissioned at Halifax. Has since operated mainly out
          of Halifax with a service life similar to *Ojibwa* and *Onondaga*.
1973   July. While working up in UK waters she had an underwater
          collision with a Royal Navy Fleet auxiliary. Sustained extensive
          damage to fin and attack periscope. No injuries to crew, whilst the
          RFA received only minor damage.
1984   Due to start her mid-life refit at Halifax dockyard.

The End . . .
The last launch — H.M.C.S. OKANAEAN.
So ends an era . . .